The Voice of the Great Spirit

The VOICE of the GREAT SPIRIT

Prophecies of the Hopi Indians

RUDOLF KAISER

Translated by Werner Wünsche

FOREWORD BY FRANK WATERS

SHAMBHALA
Boston & London
1991

For Thomas and Heidrūn

Shambhala Publications, Inc.
Horticultural Hall
300 Massachusetts Avenue
Boston, Massachusetts 02115

Shambhala Publications, Inc.
Random Century House
20 Vauxhall Bridge Road
London SW1V 2SA

© 1989 by Kösel-Verlag GmbH & Co., Munich
Foreword © 1991 by Frank Waters
Translation © 1991 by Shambhala Publications, Inc.

9 8 7 6 5 4 3 2 1

Printed in the United States of America on acid-free paper

Distributed in the United States by Random House, Inc., in
Canada by Random House of Canada Ltd, and in the
United Kingdom by the Random Century Group

Library of Congress Cataloging-in-Publication Data

Kaiser, Rudolf, 1927–
    [Stimme des Grossen Geistes. English]
    The voice of the Great Spirit: prophecies of the Hopi Indians/Rudolf Kaiser.
        p.   cm.
    Translation of: Die Stimme des Grossen Geistes.
    Includes bibliographical references.
    ISBN 0-87773-602-2 (pbk.)
        1. Hopi Indians—Religion and mythology. 2. Prophecy. I. Title.
    E99.H7K3513   1991   90-53388
    299'.784—dc20   CIP

In ancient times
a Kalapuya lay
in a grove of alder trees
near the lurking of the Santiam
and dreamt a most unusual dream.

When he awoke at night
he told the people:
"The earth beneath our feet
was completely black,
completely black
in my dream."

No one was able to say
what that signified,
that dream of our green earth—
so we forgot it.

But then the Whites came
those farmers hard as iron,
and we saw
how they tore open the earth with the plough
the pastures
the little prairies beside the Santiam.

And we knew
that we were to be part of their dream
their dream of an earth
made black forever
by the wounding plough.

—A Kalapuya Prophecy

[The Kalapuya were a grouping of several small Native American tribes in western Oregon. They are now nearly extinct, due to smallpox epidemics and warlike confrontations.]

At the beginning of Time, a buffalo was placed in the West to stem the flooding waters. Every year this buffalo loses a hair, and during every age, a leg. When he is without hair and legs the waters will flood in, and a world cycle will come to its end. It is said that the buffalo now stands on one leg and is almost bald.

—A Myth of the Oglala Sioux

[In 1980 the Oglala, a group belonging to the Teton Dakota Sioux, numbered twelve thousand people. Most of them live on the Pine Ridge Reservation in South Dakota. Their most famous Chiefs were Red Cloud and Crazy Horse.]

On the day of Purification all living things will weep. We may even see a weeping stone rolling down a mountain slope.

—David Monongye, a spiritual leader of the Hopi,
3 October 1982

Renew yourself completely every day;
do it again
and ever again
for all time.

—Inscription on a Royal Chinese bathtub

Contents

Foreword

No other world prophecy is said to be as well known as the prophecy of impending world destruction made by the Hopi Indians of Arizona. The present comprehensive study by the German writer and professor Rudolf Kaiser contains many reasons why it justifies wide notice.

The Hopi religion, like that of the ancient Mayas and Nahuas, and other contemporary indigenous native peoples, is rooted in the belief in cyclical time, in the destruction and creation of successive worlds. Hence the Hopi's predicted "Day of Purification" and the end of their present Fourth World will be followed by the creation of the Fifth World. The religion and worldview of American, European, and other Bible-oriented societies, in contrast, subscribe to a linear rather than to a cyclical concept of time. To them the dreaded global catastrophe of our thermonuclear age will be the end of the line—of our civilization, of humankind.

It is curious, as Mr. Kaiser points out, that the New Age movement, hailing the adoption of holistic-sociological values, shows some resemblance to the worldviews of native peoples and nature religions of the past.

But there are other differences more compelling. World religion prophecies pay less attention to the earth, to the environment, than do the holistical Hopis. And traditional Hopi teachings contain no prohibitive injuctions similar to those found in the Ten Commandments.

As Mr. Kaiser quotes: "There is no improvement on the Hopi way as an ethic of life. It cannot be improved upon. Take care of the Mother Earth and it will take care of you. Take care of your brother. Take what you need, but not more than you need. Share what you have. Give thanks to the spiritual source of the universe."

It is reassuring to learn there are still Hopi traditionalists who are carrying on this Way.

Frank Waters
Taos, New Nexico
October 7, 1990

Preface

In recent years European and North American specialist publications, as well as the general press, have repeatedly made reference to the prophecies of the Arizona Hopi Indians.[*]

People in the West seem to be willing to bring an open mind to the Hopi message about the "fulfillment of time," the coming "day of purification," the (possibly imminent) end of this world, and the possible establishment of a new world. In view of the threats and dangers facing the world, Westerners have become responsive to apocalyptic predictions. In this context the nuclear catastrophe at Chernobyl has helped greatly to focus our attention. As far as statements and predictions by representatives of Native American communities are concerned, it seems that the Hopi prophecy is about to replace the much-loved, much-debated, and much-maligned "Speech of Chief Seattle."[†]

Hopi religious leaders have pointed out that the catastrophe

---

[*] Buschenreiter 1983 & 1987; Doempke 1982; Clemmer 1978; Waters 1980 & 1983; Brinkerhoff 1971; Steiner 1977, 1981 & 1985; Smith 1982; Willoya & Brown 1962; Rohr 1985; Werner 1986; *Hopi Prophecy* 1988; et al.

[†] See my critical examination of the authenticity of Chief Seattle's speech (Kaiser & Kaiser 1984, 1986).

predicted by the Hopi prophecy is not inevitable, because the prophecy allows for the possibility that our world may survive, provided that humanity has a change of heart and mind and modifies its behavior accordingly. Indeed, the Hopi decided to disseminate their prophetic message throughout the world specifically to avert a global catastrophe. In consequence, a growing number of people have begun to examine the mythical ideas of that Native American nation in the hope of finding guidance toward a solution of their own problems.

In an endeavor to study at the source the historical development and the present relevance of the Hopi prophecy, I spent the greater part of the summer of 1987—with the assistance of the Deutsche Forschungsgemeinschaft, a German research organization—in the southwestern United States, particularly on the Hopi reservation, where I questioned prominent representatives of several Hopi clans from various Hopi villages about their views. For considerations of personal privacy, most of these interviewees are identified by their initials only.

In addition, I had extensive discussions with American ethnologists in Tucson, Flagstaff, Albuquerque, Santa Fe, and Denver and took the opportunity to comb the libraries of the universities and colleges in these cities for written data about the Hopi prophecy. In this regard, I owe special thanks to Professor Richard O. Clemmer-Smith of Denver University and Professor Jerrold Levy of the University of Arizona in Tucson for their extensive and generous help.

The Voice of the Great Spirit

Introduction:
The Hopi and
Their Settlements

The Hopi are a small Indian nation in the Southwest of the United States. Their tribe numbers barely ten thousand people, approximately 75 percent of whom live in twelve villages on the Hopi reservation in northeastern Arizona near the Grand Canyon. Their reservation is more remote from other centers of "white" culture and civilization than that of almost any other Native American tribe. The nearest sizeable town, Flagstaff, is over one hundred miles away.

Another important factor contributing to the isolation of the Hopi is that their reservation is completely surrounded by that of the Navajo—the largest Indian reservation in the United States, the Navajo being the most populous North American Indian tribe. Their reservation surrounds that of the Hopi like a gigantic ring and thus provides an additional buffer against the outside world.

The traditional Hopi settlements are concentrated around three table mountains that point from the Black Mesa toward the south, like the stony fingers of a gigantic hand. In the southwestern U.S. such mountains are usually designated by the Spanish term *mesa* (literally, "table"). The three table mountains of the Hopi settlements on the Black Mesa are therefore known as First Mesa, Second Mesa, and Third Mesa (counting from east to west). The Black Mesa, which forms part of the Colorado plateau, is so named because of the extensive coal deposits near its surface. It is a sacred place for the Hopi and in their mythology is described as the center of the world.

The table mountains of the desertlike region of northern Arizona are particularly arid, infertile, and stony. For that reason some of the Hopi villages are found at the foot of these mountains, but the majority of them are situated high on the mesas themselves, "near the sky." On the basis of their myths, the Hopi believe that at the beginning of this world the Great Spirit allocated these stony deserts to them as their place of settlement, thereby ordaining a modest, meager, and hardworking existence for them.

HISTORICAL DEVELOPMENT

If we wish to understand the history of the Hopi as well as their own sense of history, it is necessary to distinguish between factual historical events and their traditional history as described in their myths. While such a distinction is essential for our understanding, it is equally important to remember that the Hopi—and indeed most other Indian tribes—do not make such a clear distinction between myth and historical events, legend and fact; instead, these are frequently interwoven. History, in the last analysis, consists of stories; it is not restricted to factual and historical events but is always colored by experiences, attitudes, aims, and purposes. Seen in this way, history is the interpretation of human existence.

According to their own myths the Hopi were the first human beings on the North American continent and entered their world through an opening in the earth's crust, the so-called *sipapu*. They were the chosen survivors of the inhabitants of an earlier (subterranean) world, which fell into moral decay and therefore was destroyed by a flood. Only a few members of this earlier civilization, namely, those who had retained a pure heart, were saved and entered our world through the *sipapu*. (The earlier world destroyed by a flood was the third in a series of worlds that perished for similar reasons. Our present world, according to Hopi mythology, is the Fourth World.)

In one of the branches of the Grand Canyon there is an elevation whose highest point is marked by an opening. For a long time pious Hopi believed this opening to be the *sipapu*, the point at which their existence in this Fourth World began. However, other Hopi point out that this story of the emergence from a subterranean world should not be taken literally but understood symbolically, as the emergence of humankind from a less conscious existence into one marked by a greater consciousness. Nevertheless to this day the floor of every sacred ceremonial chamber (*kiva*) of the Hopi has a slab embedded in it, the *sipapuni*, as a symbolic representation of the spot at which humans, led by the Hopi, entered this world.

Having emerged into this Fourth World, the various clans set out on long journeys across the American continent. Like the biblical travels of the ancient Israelites through the Sinai desert, these journeys refer to a period during which the people found themselves and developed an identity. The spiral, a recurrent feature in Hopi art, is a symbolic representation of these early travels, which continue to play a central role in the consciousness of the Hopi. At the end of their travels the Hopi made their home at a place allocated to them by the Great Spirit, their present settlements.

Hopi mythology tells us that thereafter this Fourth World passed through the same stages as the three previous ones, that is, from a state of harmony to one of ambition, followed by increasing materialism and ultimately by tribulations and suffering (see the diagram on page 104). Now this Fourth World is said to be in the final stage; its end can be foreseen.

Turning from this mythological representation of history to scientific historical data, we find that the origins of this small Indian nation are somewhat obscure. There is, however, at least one point on which both myth and scientific history agree: numerous early transmigrations of peoples and tribes, thought to have been the antecedents of the Hopi, are not only referred to by the myths but are confirmed by the extensive remains of former settlements to be found throughout the southwestern United States.

Around A.D. 400 groups of basket-making people settled in the area. It is probable that the ancestors of present-day Hopi entered this Four Corners area of the Southwest around A.D. 700 from the south. This is confirmed by the fact that the Hopi language belongs to the Uto-Aztec group of languages, the center of which was located south of their present settlements.

In the eighth or ninth century these people established small villages consisting of houses with several rooms. The following four to five hundred years saw the establishment of all the large pueblos, the ruins of which continue to evoke the visitor's admiration and astonishment to this day: Mesa Verde, Pueblo Bonito in the Chaco Canyon, Betatakin, Aztec, Cortez, and many others. Even if not all the former inhabitants of these ruins were Hopi, both the clan legends and the rock drawings found in many of these ruins show that Hopi did live here over certain periods in the past. The earliest traces of Hopi culture thus date back almost thirteen hundred years. Despite the time and effort involved in the establishment of such settlements, the people who created them still were unwilling to settle there permanently: they planted cotton in the San Juan River valley and other areas throughout the Southwest, and from it wove their clothing; they cultivated corn as their main diet; they built houses in protected rock cliffs—yet again and again the Anasazi (as ethnologists now call them, using a Navajo word meaning "the old ones") left their stone dwellings and set out on yet another journey.

At the end of the thirteenth century a ten-year-long drought occurred that seems to have prompted these people to make one last journey, in the course of which some clans finally arrived at the southern edge of the Black Mesa in present-day Arizona. In this way the ancestors of today's Hopi came to settle on the southern foothills of the Black Mesa—that is, on the First, Second and Third Mesa. (However, Oraibi village was founded as early as A.D. 1150.)

One question continues to fascinate researchers: what

thoughts, aims, and considerations prompted these people so many centuries ago to choose this particular area, which has no rivers and little rainfall? It is unlikely that they were influenced by questions of fertility, since enormous sacrifices and tremendous effort are needed to wrest any kind of harvest from this stony desert. Nor is there any evidence that they were involuntarily forced to settle there under the pressure of neighboring tribes. The Hopi's own answer to the question is one in which spiritual, mythical, and cosmic concepts flow together. They say that the Great Spirit assigned this land to them to hold in trust and care for, because he wanted them to lead a simple and diligent life.

Those who have visited this sparse region know that it is of incredible beauty and majesty. The Hopi see their land as the center of the world and as a reservoir of great spiritual power, rivaled only by Tibet, that other great spiritual powerhouse. Indeed, seen from the valley floor, some Hopi villages remind one of Tibetan monasteries squatting on top of a mountain halfway between heaven and earth. Traditional Hopi continue to regard themselves as the guardians of their land and, because the land is the center of their world, also as guardians of the earth and even of the cosmos.

So ancient are the Hopi settlements in Arizona that Oraibi village on the present Hopi reservation can vie with Acoma in New Mexico for the honor of being the oldest continuously inhabited village on the North American continent. It is therefore possible that the Hopi are the bearers of the most ancient yet still enduring North American culture.

After the so-called discovery of America, the history of the Hopi Indians becomes more accessible to us. In all probability the first encounter between white people and the Hopi took place in 1540 or 1541, when Pedro de Tovar accompanied his Spanish Lord, Francisco Vasquez de Coronado, on an exploratory journey to the legendary seven golden cities of Cibola. While Coronado decided to remain in Cibola (now known as Zuni), Pedro went on to explore the province of Tusayan and became the first European to come upon the villages of the Hopi

Indians. Further contacts with the Hopi were made by Spanish explorers in 1583 (Antonio de Espejo) and 1598 (Juan de Oñate).

The first missionary attempts by three Spanish Franciscan monks led to the establishment of a mission station in Oraibi village in 1629. Subsequent tensions between the missionaries and the Hopi prompted the latter to join the great Pueblo Revolt in 1680. However, killings and expulsions of Spanish soldiers and missionaries were not confined to the Eastern Pueblos (New Mexico). They also occurred on Hopi territory.

In all probability many Hopi saw Christianity as a threat to their own highly developed religious belief, which to this day is expressed in a complex annual cycle of ceremonies. They may have felt that the loss of their own religion would sever their connection to the Great Spirit, so that they would no longer be able to protect their land and its fruits and to preserve the balance of nature.

Twelve years later another Spaniard, de Vargas, peacefully took possession of their land. The missionaries returned, and in 1700 seventy-three Hopi were christened in Awatovi village. Over the preceding years, however, the Hopi's hatred of the Spaniards' "slave church" had become so widespread that a united fighting force, assembled from several Hopi villages, destroyed Awatovi village and most of its inhabitants. This incident, dating back almost three hundred years, continues to burden the minds and consciences of many Hopi. Committed as they are to leading an upright and peaceable life, they cannot forget that they once razed one of their own villages to the ground with incredible brutality.

Thereafter the Hopi were spared further missionary attempts for more than a century. In 1822 Mexico gained its independence from Spain, and their land became part of the Mexican empire. From 1827 onward, Euro-American trappers, agents, merchants, missionaries, and settlers began to infiltrate the region. Whereas the Catholic Spaniards had endeavored to rule by the sword and the cross, the new Protestant Americans used business, trade, and money to the same end. In 1848 Mexico ceded all the land north of the Rio Grande to the United States under the treaty of Guadaloupe Hidalgo. The Hopi settlements were in that area.

Since the United States had paid fifteen million dollars for that territory, the government believed that it had also acquired a right of ownership. However, the Hopi and other North American Indians do not regard land as a commodity to be bought and sold but rather as something bestowed by the Great Spirit—a bequest to which the human community has a religious claim. We are here witnessing the encounter of two radically incompatible views. Nevertheless, for the time being, at least, the U.S. government recognized the land rights of the Indians.

In 1858 the first Mormon missionaries entered Hopi territory, only to withdraw again soon after, because of growing altercations among the Hopi (see page 66). In 1901 the first Mennonite church was built in Oraibi. The Mormons and Mennonites can be said to have been the only Christian churches whose missionary activities on the reservation met with some success. To this day, however, the majority of the Hopi have not been converted to Christianity.

In 1887 the federal government passed the General Allotment Act, also known as the Dawson Act, which envisaged that the communally owned land on Indian reservations be distributed among the families of the various tribes and henceforth owned by them. This was an attempt to acquaint the Indians with the idea of private property. In 1891 the above law was applied to the Hopi. Their communally owned land was to be divided into plots of a certain size and then distributed among the various heads of household; any remaining land was to be sold.

For the Hopi, as for many other Indians, the Dawson Act amounted to a downright sacrilege. In their view, the only "owner" of all the land was the Great Spirit, who permitted human beings to use it, provided they also take care of it in a spiritual sense. Personal land ownership was a totally alien concept to the Hopi. The only form of allocation known to them was that certain clans had the right to cultivate certain stretches of land. The Hopi, therefore, removed the rods the white surveyors had placed in the ground to parcel out the land.

The "white" Hopi agency called in the army. Six cavalry soldiers rode into Oraibi village to arrest the perpetrators. They came upon a village square thronging with a mass of people, from which two figures came forward: the first of these was dressed as Masau'u, the lord over life and death, worshiped by the Hopi also as the Great Spirit of this world. The other figure appeared in the form of Spider Woman, the ever-helpful and beneficent grandmother of many Hopi myths and legends. Both these figures then formally "declared war" on the intruders and called upon them to withdraw. Not wanting to engage in actual battle, the soldiers left Oraibi, only to return in greater strength many weeks later, when several Hopi were taken prisoner. In 1911 the plan to parcel out native Indian land was finally abandoned, so that in the end the Hopi land never was privatized.

One particular problem with which the Hopi had to contend was the infiltration of the Navajo from the surrounding territory. This infiltration began shortly after the arrival of the first Spaniards. The Navajo in question came from the north and thus were part of a native culture radically different from that of the Pueblo and the Hopi. The Navajo were livestock breeders rather than farmers; they were (and, in part, still are) seminomadic, driving their herds of sheep through the vast expanse of northern Arizona. Again and again the Navajo raided Hopi and Pueblo villages, stealing animals or part of the harvest. For that reason, relations between the Hopi and the neighboring Navajo have, for most of the time, been tense.

In 1882 the Washington authorities established the first Hopi reservation to demarcate the border between the Hopi and the adjoining Navajo. Its area—2,863 square miles—was much smaller than that traditionally claimed by the Hopi. Nevertheless, for the time being, the Hopi agreed to accept the Washington ruling.

In 1887 the first government school was opened in Keams Canyon, a settlement established by the federal authorities two years before that. Very few Hopi families were willing to send their children to that "white" educational institution. In 1890, three years after its establishment, the school was attended by only three Hopi boys. Over the next two decades (until 1911, to be exact) the white Indian administration repeatedly attempted, by the use of U.S. Cavalry troops, to capture children in the various villages or snatch them from their parents in order to take them to school. Some very old Hopi still tell gruesome stories about how they were hidden by their parents from the soldiers but in the end were discovered and forcibly taken to school.

At school the children were continually in the care of white teachers, who for the most part forbade them to speak their own language. They were forced to have their hair cut in the fashion of white children and even to dress like them. It was not uncommon for Hopi children to be kept in these boarding schools for several years without being allowed to visit their families. The explicit aim of these schools was to estrange the children from their parents' way of life. In most cases they succeeded in that goal, but these Hopi children did not adopt as an alternative the white man's ways. Caught between the standards, values, and attitudes of two so radically different cultures, they were often unable to relate constructively with any of the alternatives presented to them and ended up in a vast vacuum. The present problem of alcoholism among Native Americans—also on the increase among the Hopi—is beyond question a consequence of these developments.

Divergent attitudes to the culture of the white Americans also led to great confrontations among adult Hopi. The basic question was whether a decision to join the apparently more powerful culture of the white man and adopt his lifestyle constituted a betrayal of traditional standards and values that would take its revenge in the loss of their cultural identity. In Oraibi, the largest village on the Hopi reservation, opinions on this were so divided that two distinct factions emerged: the so-called progressives (also known as Friendlies), who were for cooperating with the whites, and the traditionalists, or Hostiles, who were opposed to such cooperation.

The struggle between the two factions literally tore the village apart. Early in September 1906 there was a real danger of physical confrontation between them. At the last moment a peaceful solution was found: on the seventh or eighth of September a line was drawn on the ground in the village and the leaders of the two factions faced each other across this line. Each placed his hands on the other's chest and—with the assistance of more or less equally strong groups of supporters—began to push, each endeavoring to cross the line. The struggle continued for several hours until, in the end, Yukioma, the leader of the Hostiles, called out, "It is done. I have been pushed back." On the evening of that day he left Oraibi in the company of his supporters. They settled about eight miles to the north of Oraibi, where they founded the village of Hotevilla.

Like the destruction of Awatovi in the year 1700, the confrontations in Oraibi are evidence of strong "splitting and disruptive tendencies," of "tendencies of dissension" within Hopi society. Again and again, within individual clans or villages, part of the group or population have split off, moved away, and founded their own community. These tendencies have of course been strengthened to an extraordinary degree by the existence of a dominant white culture. The events of 1906 nevertheless show that in accordance with the traditional Hopi principle of peaceableness, such differences can be resolved without the loss of blood.

After the 1906 confrontations, Oraibi village began to fall into ruin. In 1933 there were only 112 people still living there, and today the village gives the impression of being largely deserted. The responsibility for leading religious ceremonies passed from Oraibi to Hotevilla, which continues to be a stronghold of traditionally minded Hopi to this day. Meanwhile, it seems that Shungopovi village on the Second Mesa is about to assume a leading role in safeguarding the performance of the annual cycle of religious ceremonies.

In 1934 the federal government changed its oppressive Indian policy. President Franklin Delano Roosevelt's Indian Commissioner, John Collier, was so impressed by the richness of the various Native American cultures that, in order to preserve them, he proposed a new law, the Indian Reorganization Act. Specifically, he wanted to encourage the native people to assume responsibility for their own political organization. Among other things, this was to be achieved by establishing tribal governments (modeled on Western principles of democracy), which would decide on matters concerning the tribe in question. The ultimate aim was to abolish all cultural and religious restrictions to which the Native Americans were subject.

Unfortunately, the Hopi were one of the people chosen by Collier to demonstrate his new policy. I say "unfortunately" because traditionally the Hopi have never known any kind of political organization of their tribe as a whole. Their political, economic, and social traditions and customs do not envisage tribal structures or institutions of this kind, nor have they ever brought forth a political head or ruler over all the villages; rather, each village was completely independent in its decisions and free to determine its own future. Because of this autonomy, the inhabitants of the various Hopi villages were not inclined to place themselves under a central tribal government and that is indeed one reason why the Tribal Council established by the white authorities continues to find it very difficult to have its work recognized by the Hopi people.

In addition to the villages' autonomy, in accordance with the traditional customs of Hopi society, communal decisions must be unanimous. Against this custom the 1934 Indian Reorganization Act was based on a form of government that allowed majority decisions and the rule of the majority over the minority. Such an idea was wholly incompatible with the traditional methods of self-administration. The Hopi may have a common language, a common culture, a common religion, and common values, but never at any time have they had central political institutions of power.

Nevertheless, they were among several Native American peoples chosen for the application of the government's new and essentially well-intentioned Indian policy. In 1935 a referendum was held among the Hopi. This was followed by the drafting of a written constitution and the establishment of a Tribal Council and of a Tribal Court. Four Hopi villages that subscribed to traditional values immediately voiced their opposition to this new form of tribal administration and refused to send representatives to meetings of the Tribal Council; two villages supported the new central administration; the rest were divided or undecided. In any case, in 1936, out of altogether 4,500 Hopi, no more than 651 voted for establishing a Tribal Council, and 104 voted against it. The remainder—the vast majority of those entitled to vote—demonstrated their opposition or indifference by not participating in the election. Despite this, the result was interpreted as being in favor of a Tribal Council, which was duly established.

Since then (and possibly, to a lesser extent, before that) there has been rivalry between "traditional" and "progressive" villages. The traditionalists of all villages boycotted the Tribal Council from the outset. From 1940 onward the council did not have sufficient members to form a quorum, and in 1945 it stopped functioning altogether. In 1949–50 it was revived because there was need for a body with which concessionary leases for the exploitation of mineral resources could be concluded. While the membership of the Tribal Council rose after May 1950 to a level that was just sufficient to form a quorum, over the following years and decades the council was unable to function for several months at a time because its membership repeatedly fell below the required number.

To this day the traditionally minded villages claim the right to decide their own future. Thus the establishment of the Tribal Council, instead of helping to unite the Hopi, has unfortunately resulted in deepening divisions among them. For that reason Hopi society continues to be characterized by disruptive tendencies rather than a will or inclination to arrive at common political opinions and decisions. This is particularly regrettable in view of the discovery of enormous reserves of minerals within the territories of the Hopi reservation. These resources have become a focus of attention for energy-hungry white enterprises. In general terms it can be said that the Tribal Council and the so-called progressives support the exploitation of the extensive resources of coal on the Black Mesa, whereas the traditionalist Hopi are against it. In 1961 the Tribal Council granted a mining concession worth over three million dollars. This was energetically opposed by the traditionalists, who object to the enormous devastation of the environment and destruction of the landscape caused by strip mining. To legitimize their opposition, they stated that they saw themselves as guardians and protectors of the soil, which was sacred to them. Despite this, they failed to prevail over the Tribal Council, because the latter is considered a legally elected organ of the federal government.

The issue under dispute is the strip mining of coal on the Black Mesa approximately sixty miles north of the Hopi settlements. In 1966 the Peabody Coal Company was given permission by the Tribal Council to exploit the mineral resources of the area for a period of thirty-five years. The annual quantity of coal mined there varies between 200,000 and 1.3 million tons. Measured against the profits of the mining company, the compensation paid to the Hopi for the mining concessions must be considered minimal: since 1970 its average annual value amounted to roughly $500,000. In 1989 the Tribal Council and the Peabody Company began negotiations about the possibility of extending the area of mineral exploitation.

This revenue from concession fees has of course led to an improvement in the standard of living on the Hopi reservation. Many Hopi are now materially better off than were members of the community thirty or forty years ago. Against this profit, the traditionalists argue that the misuse and destruction of the land constitutes a sacrilege against the sanctity of life and a violation of the balance of nature. Moreover, there can be no doubt that the "progress" resulting from this "modernization" has brought in its wake a secularization of the Hopi way of life and continues to have that effect. In several Hopi villages the traditional religious ceremonies have more or less died out. The Snake Ceremony is now performed in only two villages. The Hopi language is increasingly being ousted by English, and changes in lifestyle and diet have led to an increased incidence of alcoholism and diabetes. Only on the Second Mesa are the traditional ceremonies still reasonably intact and well attended.

The mining activities cause enormous environmental damage: both the surface of the earth and the vegetation are destroyed. The groundwater level is lowered as enormous quantities of water are pumped to the surface to move the coal (mixed with water) through pipelines to the various power stations, which in turn emit vast quantities of harmful substances. In fact, the air pollution caused by one of these power stations was the only man-made phenomenon visible on earth to the astronauts involved in one of the *Apollo* space missions.

In addition, the mining activities on the Black Mesa have led to increased tension between the Hopi and the Navajo. The main deposits of coal are situated near the boundary of an area allocated to the Hopi as part of their reservation. The Navajo, whose birthrate is extraordinarily high—they are now the largest Native American tribe on the North American continent— have repeatedly infiltrated and attempted to settle in the more thinly populated parts of the Hopi reservation. In 1934 a considerably smaller area than that originally allocated to the Hopi was declared as the official Hopi reservation, and the remaining territory of their original 1882 reservation was designated as a "joint-use area" for Navajo and Hopi. Since then the number of Navajo that have settled in that joint-use area far exceeds the number of Hopi living there. This population imbalance has led to occasional incidents between the two tribes.

The Hopi Tribal Council therefore demanded the implementation of a resettlement plan to separate the Hopi from the Navajo and to determine a definite and final boundary between the two reservations. This demand lies at the heart of the so-called Hopi-Navajo dispute. The federal government supported the Hopi request, and in 1974 the U.S. Congress passed a law known as the Land Conciliation Act (Public Law 93-531) to settle the proprietory rights within the joint-use area once and for all. Specifically, that law decreed that the area hitherto used jointly by Navajo and Hopi be divided into two halves by a 300-mile barbed-wire fence—one half for the Hopi and the other for the Navajo. Any Hopi or Navajo living on the "wrong" side of this demarcation line should be resettled.

The law further stipulated that this demarcation and resettlement come into effect on 18 July 1986, which meant that by that date approximately 10,000 Navajo and about 120 Hopi were to be resettled. Near Big Mountain, a sacred elevation in the center of the present Navajo settlement area, angry Navajo women prevented—some by engaging in violent confrontations—the completion of the barbed-wire fence along the demarcation line. The traditional Navajo religion is closely tied to certain sacred places and can no longer be practiced if the people are driven from them. The Navajo therefore claimed that Public Law 93-531 was illegal because it violated the freedom of religion guaranteed by the Constitution of the United States.

Four years later this controversial issue has still not been resolved.

The Hopi like to point out that they never engaged in any warlike actions against the U.S. government, that they never were conquered by military force, and that they never signed any agreement about the surrender or transfer of land. These arguments are advanced by all traditionalist Hopi to support their claim to the entire territory formerly occupied by them, which is several times the size of the area now officially designated as their reservation.

SOCIETY AND EVERYDAY LIFE

On the reservation children are nowadays mostly born in hospitals. This makes it extremely difficult, at best, to perform the rites traditionally connected with the birth of a child. According to these rites mother and child are isolated in a darkened room of the house for the first nineteen days after birth. On the twentieth day a festive ceremony is held, during which the child is presented to the rising sun, received into the village community, and given a name. Thereafter the children, in the vast majority of cases, are raised within the extended family of the mother or the maternal grandmother.

In general, children continue to become members, and thus initiates, of a religious association—in most cases the Kachina Lodge—before reaching the age of twelve, that is, before the onset of puberty. As members of such an association they are taught the Kachina dances and their secrets and so become entitled to participate in them. Further initiations are obtained by joining the religious associations for adult Hopi. In this way a child is fully integrated into the world of adults. At the same time, children become part of a complex network of relationships that are determined by birth (enlarged family, clan, phratry, village), by their membership in various religious associations (lodge, rites and ceremonies, kiva), and by marriage (in-laws, extended family of the spouse). However, it must be said that an increasing number of adult Hopi are no longer initiated into the religious associations for adults, because they either have become converted to Christianity or grew up outside the reservation.

Although Hopi society cannot be described as strictly matriarchal, it is certainly matrilinear and matrilocal: membership in a clan is passed on via the child's mother, not via the father; in most cases an older woman will form the center of the household, which includes her own daughters, her unmarried sons, and her daughter's children. Husbands join this setup from the outside, as it were. They are part of the household but not of the same clan. Sons have a lifelong right to live in the house of their mother and occasionally return there—for instance, when their marriage breaks up. Among the Hopi the husband traditionally moves in with the wife, not vice versa. If a marriage breaks up, it is the husband who moves out, more often than not, to rejoin his mother's household.

There can be no doubt that women hold a strong position in Hopi society, because both the house and agricultural produce are traditionally considered to belong to the wife, although it is the responsibility of the husband to till the land. Not surprisingly, this traditional relationship between the sexes is increasingly threatened by the impact of the patriarchal attitudes of the white man. Nevertheless, as in the past, most Hopi women continue to perform the traditional functions within the house: they take care of the children and of older members of the extended family, prepare the meals, make pots, weave baskets, and so forth.

Practically all Hopi children have been attending the day schools that have opened on the reservation over the past decades. In all of them the working language is English. Earlier attempts by primary schools to teach in Hopi have been abandoned. The teachers are predominantly white, so that it is by no means certain to what extent they are familiar with the cultural background of their pupils. True, these Hopi children are in a better situation than those who, at the turn of the century, were dragged to school by force and detained there. In a more subtle sense, however, it can be said that these modern children, too, are caught—namely, between the traditional religious framework of their families and religious lodges and their school education, which is based on scientific principles and designed to imbue in them a Euro-American set of values.

In courtship, it is often the woman who plays an active role. Traditionally it is said that by marrying she gains a worker for the fields of her family. When women give birth, they are venerated as a source of new life. Tradition strictly rejects marriage between members of the same clan or even to a member of the father's clan. All members of a clan are considered to be related to one another, in the sense that they trace their family line back to a common forebear. Marriage within a clan would therefore be a marriage between relatives. There is even a taboo on marriage within the phratry, that is, to members of other clans closely connected with one's own clan. There are at present about forty clans on the reservation, so that a relatively large number of potential marriage partners is, as a result of these rules, excluded from the outset. These marriage taboos continue to be observed to this day, and marriages within the clan are extremely rare.

While it may seem that men play a rather peripheral role in

Hopi society, the Hopi as well as other Indian tribes observe the central principle of balance as far as relations between husband and wife are concerned. They are jointly responsible for preserving the balance of our planet, like Father Sun and Mother Earth. Men and women may perform different duties and roles, but they are considered of equal importance for the maintenance of a balanced and well-ordered universe.

The preservation of the cosmic balance is a vital determinant of Hopi thought. That balance was embedded in our world by the divine power of the creator, and the task of human beings is, therefore, to preserve or restore it if it is disturbed. Every war, every illness, every misfortune is due to a loss of cosmic balance at some point of the total framework. For the Hopi, one of the main functions of a religious ceremony is to preserve or restore that balance.

Everyday life among the Hopi is predominantly determined by the nature of their land. The climate of a dry-grass steppe and semidesert is characterized by hot summers and extremely cold winters. However, the agricultural methods used by the Hopi are, above all, imposed by the low rainfall in such areas, which results in a scarcity of water.

As far back as their history can be traced, the Hopi have always been farmers. As a rule their fields are situated in the valleys at the foot of the mesas, particularly in those regions where it is likely that the roots of plants will be able to penetrate to the groundwater. The traditional crops grown by the Hopi are corn, beans, pumpkins, cotton, and tobacco. Later they added other fruits and vegetables that were introduced by the Europeans.

Corn continues to be the staple diet of the Hopi and as such is considered sacred. Traditionally, Hopi farmers cultivate their fields of corn by a method known as dry farming, which gives a good return in such desertlike regions: using his dibble, the farmer digs a twelve- to sixteen-inch-deep hole, into which he places nine seeds of corn, "three for the worms, three to push through the hard soil, and three to grow." The plants produced by this method are fairly bushy, so that those on the edge of the field protect the rest from the strong and cold winds. The next hole is dug at a distance of six to nine feet from the previous one. A Hopi field of corn thus looks rather different from what we would normally expect to see when we think of such a field.

A good crop depends not only on the skill of the farmer but also on sufficient rain, which is prayed and danced for at the religious ceremonies of the Hopi. Because corn plants are considered to be spiritual entities, it is important that the farmer speak to them as he walks across his field. As recently as 1987 a thirty-five-year-old farmer told me that a good Hopi working on his field should carry at least a song or a kind word in his heart for the plants of corn around him. He added that according to a Hopi proverb the plants of corn know human beings better than they know the corn.

Here we have evidence of the traditional holistic Hopi view of nature: all living things in this world—not only people—are imbued with the spirit. Closely related to this is the notion of the interdependence, or interconnectedness, of everything in the universe. Humans also are embedded in this holistic and sacred framework; that is, we are not separate from nature and free to rule over it, but are part of a greater whole. Because of this interrelatedness, people are able to receive messages from other realms of existence via the spiritual links that connect all living things and can, in turn, communicate with beings of these realms through prayer and ritual dancing.

The farmers cultivate not only yellow corn but also white, red, purple, blue, and multicolored corn. Those six colors are to them symbolic of the six extensions in space—the four points of the compass plus above and below, zenith and nadir, the vortex of heaven and the center of the earth. The significance of corn is further underlined by the fact that in nearly all religious ceremonies cornmeal is strewn or sprinkled as a sign of blessing and grace, similar to holy water in Christian churches. Of particular ceremonial importance is the presentation of a fully developed cob of corn to all newborn children and to young men being initiated into a ceremonial association. Receiving such a "mother corn" is a sign of blessing.

However, fewer and fewer Hopi continue to grow their own crops, so that the size and number of cultivated fields are steadily decreasing. The Spaniards introduced animals such as sheep, donkeys, goats, and cattle, and in recent years some farmers have branched out into animal husbandry, breeding cattle and sheep. Moreover, some Hopi farmers now use small lorries and tractors on their fields and as a result have become caught up in the cash economy of the American consumer culture and thus more dependent on the U.S. economy in general.

Another important part of their economy is the Hopi arts and crafts, which include basket-making, pottery, weaving, silver work, and the carving of so-called Kachina figures. Unlike agriculture, these activities seem to be increasing.

Basket-weaving is the most ancient native craft on the North American continent. In fact, a whole cultural span, extending from 300 B.C. to approximately A.D. 700, is known as the basket-maker period. The Hopi tradition of basket-weaving is unbroken. The baskets are woven by women with a material derived from the yucca plant. They produce beautiful baskets with images of animals, clouds, lightning, and traditional geometrical patterns.

Textile-weaving is men's work among the Hopi and women's work among the Navajo. The materials used are wool and cotton. For commercial sale the Hopi weave mainly blankets, the borders of which are decorated with impressive geometrical designs. According to Hopi tradition it is the task of the bridegroom's family to weave the wedding dress of his future wife. The Hopi wife wears that same dress as a shroud when she dies.

Pottery is mainly crafted by women and dates back to the earliest beginnings of Hopi culture. Initially, the pots were for domestic use on the reservation. Today, the Hopi produce for sale a bounty of beautifully polished vessels decorated with a great variety of patterns. Although shape and decoration of the pottery are predominantly based on traditional models, it is not unknown for artists to create individual designs.

Neither the Hopi nor any other North American Indian tribe make use of the potter's wheel. Instead, the women build up the pot from a continuous roll or strip of clay, which is super-imposed on itself spirally. After that step, the bands and joints are smoothed out by hand. The adherence to this ancient method, known as coiling, and the consequent rejection of the potter's wheel seem to point to a conscious desire to keep to Indian traditions and not to succumb to the influence of white culture. For the Hopi, a pot produced on a potter's wheel is not "hand-made."

The production of silver ornaments is men's work. This craft plays an important role in securing the livelihood of many Hopi. The silversmiths use a special technique known as overlay: two sheets of silver are placed one on top of the other and welded together, after the topmost sheet has been decorated by cutting or stamping out certain patterns and motifs. Because the lower sheet has been blackened by a process of oxidation, the designs cut through the upper sheet stand out clearly and look ex-tremely effective against the dark background. The designs are usually traditional, such as clouds, lightning, corn plants, as-cending steps, Kachina figures, and rain snakes.

Next to the making of silver ornaments, the carving of Ka-china figures is today the most important craft practiced by the Hopi. In their religion, Kachinas are spiritual beings represen-tative of the powers of nature. It is said that in primordial times they taught the Hopi "all the arts they would need to survive in this world." The present role of the Kachina is to help the Hopi to make rain and to ensure the fertility of the land. Every year between December and July, religious ceremonies, known as Kachina dances, are held, at which Hopi impersonate these figures and beings. To acquaint children with the appearance of these spiritual helpers, the dancers present them—especially the little girls—with small Kachina figures carved from the root of the American cottonwood tree.

In recent years these Kachina figures have become popular artifacts and are much sought after by visitors to the reservation. They are also found in the anthropology departments of many museums throughout the world. As a result of their growing popularity, the figures have lost much of their original sacred character, because many Kachinas are now carved simply for sale. It is their retail price rather than their inherent spiritual power that now contributes to the welfare of the Hopi. In studying these figures, one can detect that their style has changed substantially over the last hundred years: the older and traditional figures appear static, their arms tucked in close to the body; the more recent ones are more dynamic, with their limbs poised in movement, perhaps portraying a dancer at one of the traditional ceremonies. Put another way, from a purely aesthetic point of view, in the course of time the figures have become ever more realistic. (The religious significance of these Kachinas is discussed in the next section, "Religious Beliefs of the Hopi.")

Another way of earning a living is to work for the Tribal Administration, and a considerable number of Hopi families have come to depend for their livelihood on this controversial institution. Lastly, some Hopi work in factories, mostly outside the reservation, while others live on welfare. There can be no question that, in general, the Hopi lead a modest and occasionally destitute existence. Young people who are unable to find work on the reservation drift off to the larger cities in the vicinity to try their luck there.

Hopi villages, whether they are situated at the foot of the mesas or on their elevations, consist of rectangular houses arranged around a central "plaza," where the dances that form part of the religious ceremonies are held. Constructed of stone and clay, the houses often have several floors and in recent years also lockable doors and glass windows. Apart from Hotevilla, Old Oraibi, and Walpi, all the villages on the reservation are connected to the electric power supply. Refrigerators, radios, and television sets can be found in most dwellings, so that the Hopi are exposed to all the temptations of a materialist civilization. Consequently, everyday life has changed considerably. Among other customs, the tradition of relating tales, myths, and legends around the fireplace in the evening is gradually dying out. At the same time white American customs are spreading. For example, the number of trailers on the reservation increases with every year.

The commercialization of formerly sacred and religious domains—clearly discernible from the changing design of the Kachina figures—appears to be an irreversible cultural trend, among both the Hopi and other North American Indian tribes. Traditionally, Native Americans do not make a clear distinction between the sacred and the profane. In other words, life and religious beliefs and practices are essentially inseparable, forming an integrated whole. The Hopi never practiced what we call "Sunday religion." Rather, everything they did had religious significance for them, because they believe—one might even say "know"—that all the things around them are pervaded by the divine spirit. Every single thing is sacred.

The characteristic dualism of Euro-American culture, with its strict distinction between the "here" and the "beyond"—and the consequent profanation of all things in and of this world—has had a growing impact on the way people on Indian reservations think and behave. The Hopi, too, are increasingly adopting a more dualistic view, in which everyday things are just ordinary objects and this world, existing in physical time and space, is no longer related to any beyond. The secularization of Hopi everyday life is gathering pace. It may be only a question of time until traditional holistic cultures like that of the Hopi—cultures that are based on beliefs very different from those prevailing in the industrialized West—succumb to the powerful assault of dualistic and materialist ideas of the dominant white culture around them. All of us, including the Hopi and other Native American communities, find it hard to resist the temptations offered by our Western consumer society.

RELIGIOUS BELIEFS OF THE HOPI

The religious practices of the Hopi revolve around the Kachinas, which, strictly speaking, are not deities, but which represent the particular spiritual essence of the various life energies and of all natural phenomena, such as minerals, clouds, winds, the stars, plants, animals, and also human beings who have died. Each Kachina has its own characteristic and unmistakable appearance. If we were to try to find their counterpart in our religious culture, we would have to say that they are rather like angels or saints.

According to traditional Hopi belief the first people on this earth were accompanied by Kachinas, who taught them the various ceremonies and crafts. Although these Kachinas subsequently left the company of people and withdrew to their present abode on the San Francisco Mountains (near the town of Flagstaff), they continue to guide the activities of the Hopi by their help and care. It is believed that they continue to spend just over half of each year, the period between December and the following July, in the Hopi villages to ensure the germination and growth of the crops, to bring rain, and to protect the people.

As the masked dances and the various ceremonies are performed, the people are able to perceive and relate to the Kachinas, who are represented by appropriately attired dancers from certain religious lodges. Pious Hopi believe that these dancers not only symbolically represent the Kachinas but are literally transformed into them as they dance, provided they do so with a pure heart and strictly observe the ritual. We have here an example of a transubstantiation somewhat comparable to the transforming of bread into the body of Christ by a Catholic priest at Holy Mass.

These Kachina dances are a particularly impressive feature of the annual cycle of religious ceremonies, the most important of which are the Wuwuchim, the Soyal, and the Powamu Ceremony. Some other rites that do not form part of the Kachina cycle—such as the Flute Ceremony and the Snake Dance Ceremony—are equally stirring. All the dances and ceremonies are publicly performed on the village plaza and are preceded by secret ceremonies in the subterranean ceremonial chambers (*kivas*) over a period that may vary from four to sixteen days. Other cults and practices connected with such ceremonies are the making and offering of prayer feathers and prayer staffs, the repeated sprinkling of corn flour as a sign of blessing, and the smoking of the ceremonial pipe to illustrate the connection between humans and the spiritual essence of things.

At all these religious gatherings the worshipers pray for spiritual and material well-being and, above all, for rain, so that the fruits of the earth may grow. In addition, the various ceremonies dramatize the unfolding of the world, the interplay of the forces of nature, and the history of the Hopi on this earth. Pious Hopi believe that the regular performance of all these ceremonies is essential for holding people and the world in balance and for restoring the cosmic balance that prevailed at the time of creation. From this point of view the ceremonies not only serve the interests of the Hopi but also benefit the world and all humankind.

The dances may continue all day and are a dramatized prayer, in which people's requests are "danced into the earth" by the ceaseless stamping of feet. For me, witnessing these dances was among the most impressive and exciting experiences of my life. I observed them from the roof of a house on one of the mesas. All around me the land extended like a boundless ocean. Over the villages and the countryside vaulted an endless blue sky. Suddenly there was the sound of clatters and rattles. Slowly the masked dancers emerged from the subterranean chambers, where for several days they had been performing secret prayers and rites. The seemingly endless row of dancers formed a circle and then the dance began, a dramatized liturgy that continued throughout the day, except for an occasional short break.

In the incessant "earthy" stamping of the feet, the sound of the pumpkin rattles, the low booming beat of the great drum, the muffled hum and murmur of the men's voices, the dancers anticipated the sound of what they prayed for: the drumming rain, the murmuring brooks, thunder and lightning, the heartbeat of the earth.

By the psychic and physical energy they emit, the dancers seek to influence the forces of nature. In their view of life, humans and nature are inextricably connected, and humans, being part of nature, are inseparable from the infinite fabric of reality. No one sharing such a view of the world could doubt that reciprocal influences are possible and, indeed, are constantly occurring in a comprehensively interwoven system.

If the dancers succeed in "attracting" rain before the dance ends—several times I was present on such occasions—their energy appears to multiply: they are experiencing the direct effectiveness of their dancing and their prayers, and they know themselves to be one with the forces of nature.

The Hopi belong to a small and steadily shrinking number of Indian tribes for whom such ceremonies still serve their original religious purpose and have not yet become a tourist attraction. For that reason, it is strictly forbidden (since 1910) to take photographs or make any other kind of record of a sacred dance. However, even on the Hopi reservation, despite its remoteness, the impact of the dominant white culture is so strong that the annual cycle of sacred ceremonies has begun to disintegrate. The Snake Ceremony, for instance, is now held in only two villages, which, moreover, take turns in performing this annual sacred ritual. Very few Hopi villages still manage to adhere to the complete cycle of ceremonies throughout the year.

The Hopi dances (including the masked dances) on the village plazas are open to white visitors, unlike the masked dances of the Eastern Pueblo Indians of New Mexico, who are not of Hopi origin. In fact, the Pueblo do not allow any white observers or spectators at any of their masked dances. In the case of the Hopi, only the Snake Dance—an ancient ritual formerly performed by many tribes during which the dancers handle living snakes—has been closed to white spectators since 1986. The Hopi are the only Indian tribe that continues to perform this ceremony in the whole of North and Latin America.

In accordance with their religious traditions, the Hopi see themselves as guardians of their land and, by extension, of humankind. Since they exercise this guardianship mainly by performing their traditional ceremonies, these traditions should not be allowed to die out. However, for Hopi in the employ of white companies, it is extremely difficult because of the inflexible daily or weekly work rosters to get time off to fulfill their religious tasks and duties.

In addition to the spirits known as Kachinas, the god Massau'u plays an important role in Hopi religion. As the Lord of Fire and of Death, he is also Lord of the Fourth World, our present world. Being lord over all life on this earth, Massau'u has, moreover, increasingly assumed the role of the Great Spirit. It was he who received the first people, the Hopi, as they emerged from the Third into this Fourth World. He gave them permission to settle there and at the same time ordained a way of life for them: "If you are willing to live as I do and follow my instructions, the life plan I shall give you, you can live here with me and take care of the land, leading a long, happy, and fruitful life." This life plan took the form of a drawing that the Great Spirit, by the power of his breath, etched upon sacred stone tablets, which have since been passed on from generation to generation by the Bear Clan and the Fire Clan. Massau'u is thus the founder of Hopi culture.

Another important figure in Hopi mythology is Spider Woman, or Spider Grandmother. She is an embodiment of the "good mother" and, in fact, of justice, of goodness in general, and of all earthly knowledge. She helped to make the world habitable for human beings and is the driving force behind discoveries and inventions. By her grandmotherly love she helps all the Hopi, but in particular her two grandsons, the moody war gods Püánghoya and Palôngahoya, to overcome evil powers, demons, and evil thoughts.

In understanding the significance of Spider Woman, we may arrive at a better understanding of Hopi cosmology, in which all reality is interwoven like the net of a spider's web. The spider brings its web forth from its own body, its own being. Spider Woman is thus not symbolic of a transcendent creator goddess remote from her creation but an image of the energy and power immanent in a continuously developing cosmos. Her two grandsons are stationed at the two poles of our earth, where they hold the earth's axle in balance and ensure its regular rotation. If they are negligent in their duties, they may create imbalances such as earthquakes. The two twins are a personification of the basic idea of cosmic balance.

Unlike these helpful and comprehensible embodiments of spiritual energies, Tawa, or Táiowa, the creator god of Hopi mythology, is less easily understood. He is the primordial spiritual nature, the spiritual aspect of existence before there was space and time. Through him the ordering power of the universe, Sotuknang, came into being. This universe, as mentioned before, has already passed through three worlds or earth ages that all ended in catastrophe, because their inhabitants ignored the will of the creator. In each case, a few just people survived the end of their world to establish the next world. Because of the recurrence of similar cycles of development in these earlier worlds, the Hopi are able to determine what stage of development our world is now in and how near to its end that world is.

Hopi religion sees the cosmos as a complex network of natural, and at the same time spiritual, forces and energies, which ideally hold each other in balance, as intended by the creator. Without this balance, life on earth will ultimately cease. To preserve and continuously restore it whenever it is disturbed at any point in its vast interconnected structure is thus vital. The Hopi believe that preserving and restoring the cosmic balance is their first task, which they perform by conducting their sacred ceremonies and by leading a just and peaceable life in accordance with the instructions given them by the Great Spirit.

Many Hopi are convinced that if the Hopi religion is forced to succumb to the onslaught of Euro-American culture, there will be no one left to hold the cosmos in balance and this Fourth World, too, will then end in catastrophe. The signs of increasing disorder and confusion are all around us. The Hopi word for a world that threatens to escalate out of balance is *Koyaanisqatsi*.

Traditionally minded Hopi believe that this balance is also endangered whenever Hopi convert from their religion to Christianity. A similar threat arises from the spread of technology and the materialistic lifestyle of white Americans. In this context, the destruction of the land and the natural as well as social environment, due to the activities of white mining companies, are cited as an example of this. Conservative Hopi are convinced that the impending catastrophe can be averted only by the preservation of traditional Hopi virtues and a life lived in conformity with the Hopi life plan and in peace with nature. However, there are others who are inclined to make use of the good things the white man's culture has to offer and who try— if at all possible—to remain faithful to the traditional Hopi values.

The Hopi believe in a life after death. Their afterlife is not dissimilar to this world but is based in every sense on the principle of opposites; that is, when someone dies on earth someone is born in the underworld and vice versa. When it is winter on earth, it is summer in the underworld; our day is their night. This other world is thus a kind of mirror image of our world, and both worlds stand in close, mutually supportive relationship to each other. The dead have not passed away forever but can be addressed and prayed to by the living.

In Hopi language the word *Hopi* means something like "those who are honest, upright, decent, at peace with humankind and nature, and live in accordance with the instructions of the Great Spirit." The word *Hopi* thus initially designated an ethical or moral quality, and it still does. The people of the Hopi nation see their name as an example, as something to live up to, and they continue to encourage their young people to follow the example.

Nevertheless, as our brief survey of Hopi history shows, they have not always behaved peaceably. Moreover, they do occasionally beat or behave violently toward their spouses, children, and animals. No one remains peaceable at all times and under all circumstances. Nor do we know of any exclusively peaceable human societies or communities. Hopi society, too, is marked by occasional tensions and violence.

It is worth noting, however, that in the vast majority of cases the Hopi seem to have succeeded in resolving such tensions and violent tendencies by agreeing that groups of people holding totally irreconcilable views should separate. The division of

Oraibi village in 1906 is one well-known example of this. Again and again groups of Hopi who found themselves in profound disagreement decided to separate, and irreconcilable arguments within a clan have frequently led to the formation of two new clans. These divisive tendencies are, once again, clearly visible in the mutual opposition between the traditionalists and the progressives. Readers must judge for themselves whether such a way of handling potential strife—by division, separation, and departure of one of the parties involved—could serve as a model for dealing with our own culture's tendencies toward violent confrontation.

Although the Hopi are one of the most remote Indian people in the United States, they have in all probability been studied and investigated by ethnologists to a greater extent than other Native American tribes. For over a hundred years, many anthropologists and ethnologists have studied the culture of these open-hearted and largely peaceable people. Their publications fill whole shelves in our libraries and thus provide us with a rich corpus of scientific findings and data about an Indian people that lives in an extremely remote region—a people, moreover, whose religious and social traditions are still reasonably intact.

It certainly appears worthwhile—and may well be essential— that we in the West listen to what the Hopi have to say about our present world, in which the survival of humankind, threatened by ecological destruction and military annihilation, has become the most urgent question facing us. In this context, the Hopi prophecy can be seen as a tradition from which people of our culture—and indeed the world as a whole—might receive guidance and help. This book is an attempt to examine that prophecy in some detail.

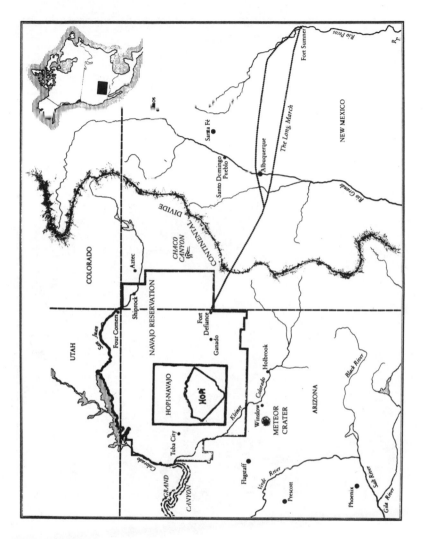

The "Four Corners," in the southwestern area of the United States

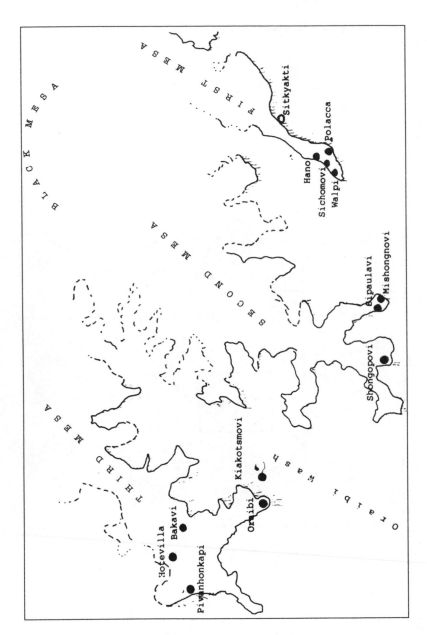

The Three Mesas of the Hopi

Walpi village on the First Mesa

1

What Prompted the Religious Leaders of the Hopi to Publish Their Prophecies?

In 1947, two years after the end of the Second World War, a religious gathering was held in Shungopovi village on the Hopi reservation, at which religious leaders of the Hopi discussed the postwar state of our world. A representative of the Bluebird Clan informed the assembly that as a young man, during his training as a religious leader, he had been told that if a "gourd of ashes" were to fall from the sky, he should publicly proclaim the hitherto secret teachings, prophecies, and traditions of the Hopi nation. Other clan leaders claimed to have been given similar instructions concerning the future publication of their traditional teachings and prophecies. Soon general agreement was reached that the words *gourd of ashes* could be a reference only to the atomic bombs dropped in 1945 on Hiroshima and Nagasaki. The white people, by virtue of their technology, had at their disposal a weapon capable of destroying their own civilization and, in fact, every vestige of human culture on earth. Furthermore, it was noted that other predictions have been fulfilled: prior to the final day of purification, humankind would suffer two violent eruptions (the two World Wars); vehicles without wheels would travel along roads in the sky; and the surface of the earth would be covered by a vast "cobweb" that would enable people to communicate with each other over long distances. Many of those attending the assembly felt that the Last Days had come—and with them, the time to make public that which had been kept secret.

It is possible, however, that the decision to publicize the ancient prophecies was influenced by yet another factor: over the previous ten years the Christianization and acculturation of the Hopi to the white man's way of life had made great inroads throughout the reservation. As a result, the threat to the traditional Hopi way of life was greater than ever before. The leading proponents of the traditional culture of the Hopi people may therefore have felt that the time had come to oppose this trend as energetically as possible, in order to protect their way of life from extinction. The 1947 assembly of Hopi religious leaders may be seen as an occasion at which the movement guided by, and adhering to, the values and customs of traditional Hopi culture and religion emerged. In this context, the ancient Hopi prophecies clearly held an important place.

This first gathering was followed by another religious meeting in the subterranean ceremonial chambers (*kivas*) of the Hopi, and in 1948 a conference of village elders and the religious leaders of all Hopi villages was held—again at Shungopovi. For four days the participants discussed the religious significance of their land to the Hopi, as well as the history, traditional obligations, religious teachings, and prophecies of the various clans. Several spokesmen and interpreters were entrusted with the task of proclaiming all relevant information and decisions to the world at large. The best known of these spokesmen is Thomas Banyacya of the Coyote Clan. Although he is not a religious leader, his name appears—either as spokesman or translator— at the foot of many letters and documents made public by the Hopi since 1948. Apart from him, other long-standing religious leaders, such as David Monongye, James Kootshongsie, and, above all, Dan Katchongva, have come to be recognized as highly articulate propagators of Hopi mythology and the Hopi prophecies.

In 1949 a group of Hopi elders for the first time addressed a joint communication to the then president of the United States, Harry S. Truman, in which they said:

> This land is a sacred home of the Hopi people and all the Indian race in this land. . . . The boundaries of our empire were established permanently and were written on Stone Tablets which are still with us. Another was given to the White Brother, who . . . will return with His Stone Tablet to the Hopis. . . . The White Brother will restore order and judge all people here. . . . This land is not for leasing or for sale. This is our sacred soil. . . . Our tradition and religious training forbid us to harm, kill and molest anyone. We, therefore, object to our boys being forced to be trained for war to become murderers and destroyers.

That letter contained important elements of the Hopi prophecies and was signed by three village elders, nineteen religious leaders, and several other spokesmen and interpreters (compare Clemmer 1978, p. 71).

Over the following years a considerable number of such communications and messages were dispatched from the Hopi reservation to subsequent U.S. presidents, as well as to the United Nations, various international congresses, and selected individuals. Hopi representatives, both singly and in groups, undertook long journeys to plead the cause of the Hopi people. On several occasions they tried to present their petitions in person at the United Nations headquarters in New York, albeit without much success. James Kootshongsie and Thomas Banyacya lectured in various European cities on the worldview and prophecies of the Hopi, for example, 1983 in Bonn, as recently as 1988 in Berlin (Banyacya), and 1987 in Geneva (Kootshongsie). There was even an attempt to invite the Dalai Lama to a world conference of religious leaders to be held on the Hopi reservation. He was unable to accept the invitation but had a meeting in Los Angeles with several religious leaders of the Hopi.

Other important events in this context were the Hopi Hearings held in 1955 and the Meeting of Religious People convened in 1956. The Hopi Hearings were conducted by the "white"

Indian Administration "to hear the problems of the Hopi." The Meeting of Religious People was called by the religious leader Dan Katchongva. At both these gatherings the Hopi myths and Hopi prophecies were again publicly proclaimed and used as an aid to interpret the present world situation. In 1957, the more important speeches of the Meeting of Religious People were published as a brochure, which contributed considerably to the spread of these ideas.*

Further brochures and short treatises on the subject followed, such as Dan Katchongva's *From the Beginning of Life to the Day of Purification—Teachings, History and Prophecies of the Hopi People* (1972) and *The Essence of Hopi Prophecy* (1981) by Thomas Tarbet, a white American and an authority on Hopi mythology. All these publications deal with the mythical thinking of the Hopi, their ideas and beliefs about the beginning of this world, the instructions given to them by the Great Spirit, their way of life, their present situation, and their prophecies about an awesome purification of humankind and the end of this world. Clearly, the Hopi prophecies do not form a separate, or isolated, tradition but are part of Hopi mythology. Embedded in the traditional teachings of the Hopi people, they make up the "contemporary" finale of mythology, as it were. While the earliest traditions of Hopi mythology—the Creation myths—tell us how our world came to be, the prophecies deal with the future and the *end* of this world. Both are concerned with what is essentially beyond experience and thus subject to interpretation.

However, since the end of the Second World War, the Hopi prophecies have come to be considered so important that— although part of the general body of myths—they have assumed a certain independence and have become central to everyday political events and to discussions about current cultural change.

The Hopi prophecies—just like their biblical counterpart—do

---

* W. Bentley, C. Carpenter, "Hopi Meeting of Religious People," Hotevilla, Arizona, 1957.

not describe or predict history "in advance," but rather, they are an attempt to interpret the meaning of history and its potentialities for good or ill from a religious or theological point of view.

2

The Hopi Prophecy in Light of Recent Publications

I have chosen two characteristic extracts to show how the Hopi prophecy has been perceived and evaluated in numerous articles and publications during the last three decades.

The first is short and is a statement made in 1969 by a veteran religious leader of the Hopi on their reservation during a conversation with the American ethnologist Richard O. Clemmer:

> When I was a boy, down in the field, my father say someday the earth would turn around, turn over. . . . He say when that happen that be the Purification Day. The sky get black and we be crawling around just like ants—can't see things come—like lots of airplanes block the sun and drop lots of kind of like rain. There be those four—rain, earth turning over, ocean coming up, and thunder . . . it happen all over earth, to all peoples. (Clemmer, *Koyaanisqatsi*, n.d.)

The second extract is from a letter sent by Thomas Banyacya of Oraibi, Arizona, on 12 January 1961 to a woman in Germany:

> All Indians, as you well know, in this country have suffered untold sufferings under the dictatorial rules of Spain, Mexico and the United States Government. It is still going on not so much by acts of violence, but by subtilty, fraud and intimidation. Today the

majority of the Indians have lost most of their homelands, their way of life is completely destroyed and many of them are now Indians without a country! All [this is] due to the fact that [the] red man wants to be what they are: to live their way of life and to hold in common all land in accordance with the Great Spirit's instructions!

I was one of the six-man-delegation who went to the United Nations in New York two years ago. As interpreter for traditional Hopi leaders I had to go with them on their historic trip to fulfill their sacred mission in line with their ancient instructions. Because of the knowledge of these prophecies the Hopi leaders felt it was time to go East to the edge of our mother land where it had been foretold "a House of Glass or Mica would stand at this time, where great leaders from many lands would be gathered to help any people who are in trouble."

Therefore the Hopi leaders have to go East to the United Nations for three main reasons:

1. to look for his true white brother;

2. to seek real justice for all Indian brothers and for all good people in this land;

3. to warn the great leaders in [the] Glass House of [the] coming purification day which has been prophecied to come to this land of the red man, when the evil ones among [the] white race bring all life back to the day before the great flood, which has destroyed all life in another world, the underworld.

Our forefathers have all expressed their sincere faith that when [the] Hopi at this time come before the leaders in [the] Glass House at least one or two or three leaders or nations would hear and understand. For it is told that they should know these ancient instructions too. That upon hearing the message of Hopi they would immediately act to correct many, many wrongs being done to the chosen race, the red man, who was granted permission to hold in trust all land and life for the Great Spirit.

Hopi leaders also know that they may be denied the opportunity to deliver their message. They may find the door of the United Nations closed to them. If this happens, you will know that the great leaders in the Glass House are looking to and working for evil ones among all people. When the great leaders in the Glass House do not listen to the voices of the Hopi [the] peaceful one[s], they have fulfilled one of the prophecies which said: "When great leaders in the Glass House refuse to open the door to you when you stand before it at that day: Do not be discouraged or turn about on the path you walk, but take on more courage, determination and be of great rejoicing in your hearts. For on that day the white race who are on your land with you have cut themselves from you and thereon lead themselves to the greatest punishment at the day of purification. Many shall be destroyed for their sins and evil ways. The Great Spirit has decreed it and no one can stop it, change it or add anything to it. It shall be fulfilled!"

Briefly [the] Hopi ancient teachings and prophecy:

[The] Hopi believe[d] that [the] human race has passed through three stages of life since its origin. . . . At the end of each stage human life has to be purified or punished by certain acts of the Great Spirit, due mainly to the corruption, greed and turning away from the Great Spirit's teachings. The last great destruction was by flood which destroyed all but a few faithful ones.

Before this happened, these few faithful ones asked and received a permission from the Great Spirit to live with him in this new land. [The] Great Spirit said: "It is up to you, if you are willing to live my poor, humble and simple life. It is hard and if you are willing to live according to my teachings and instructions and will never lose faith in the life I shall give you, you may come and live with me." The Hopi and all who were saved from the great flood made a sacred covenant with the Great Spirit. They made an oath that they will never turn away from him.

Now the Great Chieftain who led the faithful one[s] to this new land and life was a Bow clan and he had two sons who were of the same mother. . . . It was to these two brothers [that] a set of sacred stone tablets were given and both were instructed to carry them to a place the Great Spirit had instructed them. The older brother was to go immediately to [the] East, to the rising [sun] and upon reaching his destination must immediately start back to look for his younger brother who shall remain in the land of the Great Spirit. His mission was to help his younger brother to bring about purification day at which time all wicked [ones] or wrongdoers shall be punished or destroyed, after which real peace, brotherhood and everlasting life shall be brought about. He will restore all land back to his brother from whom the evil one[s] among [the] white man shall have taken from him. He will come also to look for [the] sacred stone tablets and to fulfill the sacred mission given him by the Great Spirit.

The younger [red] brother was instructed to cover all land, to mark well his footprints as he goes about in this land. Both of the brothers were told that a great white star will appear in the sky as the people moved about in this land and other lands. They were told that when that happened all people shall know that [the] older brother has reached his destination and thereupon all people were to settle wherever they happen to be at that time. They were to settle permanently until [the] older brother, who went East, returned to him.

It is said that the older brother after many years may change in color of skin which may become white but his hair will remain black. He will also have the ability to write things down and will therefore be the only one to read the Sacred Stone Tablets. When he returns to this land and find[s] his younger brother, these Stone Tablets will be placed side by side to show to all the world that they are true brothers. Then great judgment and punishment will take place for he will help his younger brother to bring about real justice for all Indian brothers who have been mistreated since the coming of the white man upon our motherland.

Many prophecies concerning the time of his coming [are] well known to the Hopi leaders; [a] few of which are: when the lives of all people in this land are so corrupted, people turn to material things and not to spiritual teachings; and when the evil ones among [the] white race [are] about to destroy the land and life of [the] Hopi and other Indian brothers; when the road in the sky has been fulfilled; and when the inventing of something [has taken place], in Hopi tongue a gourd of ashes: one of which, when [it] fall[s] upon the earth will boil everything within [a] great area of land where no grass will grow for many years; when [the] leaders turned to [the] evil one instead of [the] Great Spirit.

Every Hopi village has some knowledge of this prophecy. It was in this manner [that] Oraibi and Shungopovi were settled permanently in this area which is a desert without any water to irrigate this land; for in this way the Hopi will never forget the teachings and instructions of the Great Spirit.

It is known that our true white brother when he comes will be all-powerful and he will wear [a] red cap or red cloak. He will be large in population; [he] belongs to no religion but his very own.

He will bring with him the sacred Stone Tablet. Great will be his coming. None will be able to stand against him. All power in this world will be placed in his hand and he will come swiftly and in one day get control of this whole continent. Hopi has been warned never to take up arms.

With him [the older brother] there will be two great ones, both very intelligent and powerful, one of which will have a symbol or sign of [the] swastika, which represents[s] purity and is male.

Also he will have this symbol or sign which also represent[s] purity and is female, a producer of life; the red lines in between the sign represent [the] life blood of a woman.

The third one, the second one of the two helpers to our true white brother, will have a sign of a symbol of [the] sun. He, too, will be many people and very intelligent and powerful. We have in our sacred Kachina Ceremonies a gourd rattle which is still in use today and upon which [are] painted sign[s] of these two powerful helpers of our true brother. It looks something like this:

This, the Hopi say, represent[s] the world. And when the time of [the] purification day is near, those with these signs, [the] swastika and [the] sun, will shake the earth first for a short period of time in preparation for the final day of purification. They will shake the earth two times; then it will fall upon the third one with whom these two will join, and together they will come as one to bring on [the] purification day and to help his younger brother who waits in this land.

It is also prophesied that if these three fail to fulfill their mission then the one from the West will come like a big storm. He will be many, many people, and [an] unmerciful one. When he comes he will cover the land like ants. The Hopi people have been warn[ed] not to get up on housetops to watch as he will come to punish all people. We do not yet know who this man is from the West, only that he will have a very large population.

Then if none of these fulfill their mission in this life the Hopi leaders will place their prayer feathers to the four corners of the earth in an appeal to the Great Spirit. He will cause the lightning to strike the earth people. Only the righteous ones will revive. Then, if all people [have] turned away from the Great Spirit [he will cause] the great waters to cover the earth again. We humans shall have lost the chance to enter everlasting life. They say the ants may inhabit the earth after that.

But if the three fulfill their sacred mission and if one or two or three Hopi [have] remained fast to the last on these ancient teachings or instructions then the Great Spirit, Massau'u, will appear before all that will be saved and the three will lay out a new life plan which leads to everlasting life. This earth will become new as it was from the beginning. Flowers will bloom again, wild game will come home and there will be [an] abundance of food for all. Those who are saved will share everything equally. They will all recognize [the] Great Spirit and they may intermarry and speak one tongue. A new religion will be set if the people desire it.

This is what the Hopi know and wait for by adhering to this way of life; and in spite of hardship[s] they have been faithful up to this day. For they are upholding this land and life for all righteous people.

Now the evil white man is about to take away our last remaining homeland. We are still being denied many things including the right to be as Hopis and to make our livelihood in accordance with our religious teachings. The Hopi leaders have warned leaders in [the] White House and the leaders in [the] Glass House, but they do not listen.

We now stand at the crossroad whether to lead ourselves into ι ιι ιlιιϧlhιϧ lιfu υι [ιιιtυ] tötAl desLιucLιon. The Hopi still holds the sacred Stone Tablets and is now wait[ing] for the coming of his true White Brother. (From Clemmer, 1978, pp. 47 ff.)

3

Prophecy Rock

Many Hopi believe that the prophecy under discussion is reproduced in the form of a rock drawing on the Hopi reservation close to Oraibi village. A faithful copy, made by a Hopi, of the drawing found on Prophecy Rock is reproduced in the accompanying illustration.

From the information I gathered on the Hopi reservation in the summer of 1987, it seems certain that the drawing itself was engraved on that rock no earlier than some time between 1890 and 1905. During a conversation I had in 1987 with Tom Tarbet, an authority on the Hopi, he expressed the view that the drawing was made in 1904 either by Qötsiventewa (of the Bow Clan) or by Wik-vaya (of the Sand Clan). The last-mentioned is the grandfather, on his mother's side, of John Lansa from Old Oraibi.

So, despite the fact that this drawing is situated near Oraibi, the oldest Hopi village, and that it is engraved on a huge free-standing vertical boulder overlooking a large area of Hopi territory and faces the rising sun, it is, from a historical point of view, not as significant as the verbal tradition of the prophecy and the sacred tablets.

Nevertheless, when we compare the Prophecy Rock drawing with the oral tradition of the Hopi prophecy, a possible—albeit

inconclusive—convergence between the two emerges. For instance, the figure in the bottom left-hand corner could be interpreted as Massau'u, the Great Spirit, who taught the Hopi way of life to the people as they emerged from the underworld (represented by the vertical line beside Massau'u). The sun (or moon) and star (or perhaps a symbol of the four points of the compass) to the right of that vertical line could be seen as symbols of cosmic energies connected with that way of life, which is characterized by its close links with nature, the earth, and the obligation to take care of the soil and lead a modest, diligent, humble, and simple life. The fact that this ideal life plan is not adhered to by everyone is indicated by the parallel lines extending toward the right of the drawing. According to Dan Katchongva, "There are two ways they can follow—the way of the Great Spirit or the way of the white man." According to such an interpretation, the lower of the two lines stands for the spiritual path, the right way of the Hopi. Here the corn grows, people attain a ripe old age (as indicated by the stick one of the figures uses to support itself), and the path itself seems to be without end, because that lower line runs up to the very edge of the rock. Opinions are divided as to whether the figure shown on the path depicts simply an old person or whether it is a representation of Massau'u returning at the end of this world. Yet another interpretation is that the drawing shows Massau'u at the beginning and end of the way of life of the Hopi.

The upper line is interpreted by traditional Hopi as symbolizing the materialist path, the wrong way of life—the way of the white man, which an increasing number of Hopi have adopted. The vertical connections between these two life paths indicate that it is always possible to cross from one way of life to the other, in either direction. According to the traditional legends, those that stray from the Hopi way of life (to follow the path of the white man) will be judged at the end of time. For that reason it is said that the figures were originally depicted without heads, because the ancient myths state that on the day of purification, that is, at the end of this world, evildoers will be decapitated. The drawing also makes it clear that the materialist path has no future, because after zigzagging erratically, it comes to an end before it reaches the edge of the rock. This accords with the prophecy that the white man will destroy himself and the world, after causing many difficulties for the Hopi and attempting to make the Hopi abandon their way of life. The zigzagging upper line could therefore also symbolize the disappearance of order and the tribulations and sufferings that will precede the end of time, as depicted by the Hopi word *Koyaanisqatsi*.

The oral tradition about the rock drawing often interprets the first two circles of the lower path, the Hopi path, as the first two of three "shakings-up," which the world will suffer in our time, that is, as the First and Second World War. The third circle, which is not completely closed, could therefore point to the third great catastrophe, the final purification. At the Hopi Meeting of Religious People in Hotevilla village on 4 August 1956 (see

Bentley & Carpenter), Dan Katchongva, a traditional religious leader of the Hopi and public proclaimer of Hopi prophecies, stated: "Another prophecy that has been passed down to us is that there will be three great wars which will take place on this earth. Someone will start the war and it will go a little way and it will come to an end; another person will start it again and then it will stop for a little while; then the third one will come and it will not stop until everything is purified on this earth and the wicked ones destroyed."

Some traditional Hopi thus interpret the Prophecy Rock drawing in this, or a similar, way. Dan Katchongva's book, *From the Beginning of Life to the Day of Purification*, contains the following passage: "The Great Spirit obligated us to follow his way of life. He gave the land to us to use and care for through our ceremonial duties. He instructed us and showed us the road plan by which we must govern our lives. We wrote this pattern on a rock so that we would always be reminded to follow the straight road. The Hopi must not drift away from this road or he [the Great Spirit] will take this land away from us. This is the warning given by Massau'u" (1977, p. 15f.).

A similar interpretation is presented by Thomas Banyacya in his own drawing, based on the Prophecy Rock drawing, reproduced in the accompanying illustration. To his copy of the Prophecy Rock drawing, Banyacya has added several ancient Hopi symbols, the meaning of which is described in chapter 2. He explains his drawing as follows:

> Our Hopi history and knowledge tells us that at the time of emergence we met the spirit who owns this world. He met us and we asked him to be our leader. He refused, saying that we had our own mission to fulfill before he would consider becoming our leader. He set this life out for us. He gave us instructions. This is symbolized by him holding the line [in his hand].
>
> Now the circle at the bottom of the drawing symbolizes the physical world and creation. We went forth into our journeys [clan migrations]. We reached a certain point in time, who knows, maybe a thousand years [ago]. There we were met by Massau'u again. Here he gave us more instructions. To the Hopis he gave a

path of life to follow. This is shown by the straight line that goes across. To the white brother he gave different instructions. The white brother went up and the Hopis went another direction.

Now at this second meeting with Massau'u, he told us that within the life of this current world, there would be three phases of life where the whole world would be shaken up. Three nations would rise up and shake the world. This we interpret to mean world wars. Now up at the left side we see a symbol. This is what is painted on the Hopi ceremonial rattles that are given to children.

The rattle symbolizes the world. The painting on the rattle shows the symbols of the countries that would shake the world three times. I think that the swastika in the middle symbolizes the German people, who have that for a symbol. They brought the United States into the First and Second World Wars. The sun symbol signifies the Japanese people who brought the United States into the Second World War. Pasivaya, an old religious leader from Shipaulovi, told me that the third nation to rise up would have its national symbols in red. The people would wear red caps or red robes. So the world has been shaken up twice already. There is one more war left.

So after the second meeting with Massau'u the white brother went on his way and we [the Hopis] went on our way, according to instructions. But it was told that we would meet again someday, that this white brother would come back to purify us so that we would become one people again. So on the top, the line means this—it shows the journey of this white brother. In the life of the white brother he would show himself to be clever and gifted. He would invent many scientific things.

So the first three figures shown on the top line symbolize the stages of the white man, his scientific advancement, from the carriage to the automobile to the airplane. The circles right underneath the figures prophesy the three gourds of ashes that would fall on earth. The first and second circles are interpreted to mean the bombs that fell on Japan in World War II. The four headless figures on top show our Hopis who have become like the white man. These are Hopis who have forsaken their Life Plan and who have become like the Pahana [white man]. They have fallen for their [the white people's] way of life—the easy life, the modern conveniences—and do not care for Hopi life any more. These Hopis will say to other Hopis to follow their ways. Now if all Hopis fall for this trap, then life will be like the line going up [toward the upper right-hand corner of the drawing]. It will be up and down, turmoil, earthquakes, floods, drought. The old people say we are at this stage of life now.

But it is prophesied that a phase of life will come when those Hopis who have become like the white man will realize their wrong doings and attempt to join again the Hopis who are holding on. This is symbolized by the line going down, back to the Life Plan of the Hopis. Now if this happens, then there will be times of unity, of all Hopis working together. We would have then come back to this Life Plan set out by the Great Spirit for us. This is symbolized by the circle [life] and the corn.

Now it is foretold that we would meet up with Massau'u one more time [purification?] as symbolized by the figure. He will judge us and if we are deserving to go on with him, he will accept to be the leader of the Hopis. And thereafter we will have a happy life.

As you see, the simple drawing that I have explained to you talks about the whole world from beginning to end. (*Hopi Mental Health Conference Report*, 1982, p. 40f.)

This shows that different Hopi commentators understand and interpret the Rock drawing in their own way. There appears to be no generally accepted uniform interpretation. While Banyacya considers the white brother to be identical with white people in general, some Hopi would disagree with such an interpretation. Many have pointed out that any interpretation of the Prophecy Rock drawing must, of necessity, be based on subjective judgments, since no one knows exactly what the drawing signified to the person that made it.

Nevertheless, the following considerations do seem to indicate that the Prophecy Rock drawing is a graphic representation of two opposing ways of life. During the period from which the rock drawing dates (1890–1905), the inhabitants of nearby Oraibi village were extremely preoccupied with whether they should totally reject the culture of the white man. In 1906, the differences of opinion about this problem led to a breakup of the village. Approximately half its inhabitants left Oraibi to establish another village some miles away, which became known as Hotevilla. Those confrontations eventually led to the foundation of three more villages—Bakabi, Moenkopi, and Kykotsmovi. Those inhabitants of Oraibi who were against any kind of cooperation with the white man may well have considered the preceding interpretation of the drawing as correct, because it implies that the drawing has a didactic intention—namely, to remind the other inhabitants of the Hopi prophecies and to present them with a pictorial image of the two ways of life open to them. In any case, there is little doubt that the figure in the bottom left-hand corner represents Massau'u, as he receives the Hopi that emerge from the underworld in search of an abode in this world.

At the same time we should not forget that the verbal tradition of the prophecy, being central to Hopi mythology, is in no way dependent on the rock drawing, and is, of course, much older.

During a conversation at his house on 13 August 1987, Tom Tarbet surprised me again when he mentioned that a Canadian rock drawing was similar to the one on the Hopi Prophecy Rock and was, in all probability, also of Native American origin. He said that an acquaintance of his had informed him about a rock known as "Sarcee Prophecy Rock" in Alberta (Canada), near the reservation of the Sarcee Indians in the vicinity of Calgary, and sent him a copy of it.

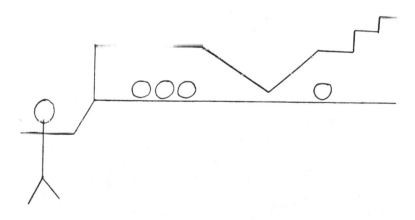

The similarity of this drawing to that found on the Hopi Prophecy Rock is unmistakable. Like the Hopi drawing, it features the Great Spirit Massau'u and the two lines, which can be interpreted as representing two distinct ways of life. Although at one point the two lines approach each other quite closely, they then grow farther and farther apart. Instead of the three circles in the Hopi rock drawing, alleged to symbolize two occasions in which our world would be "shaken up" and the impending final purification, the Sarcee drawing contains four circles. Finally, there are no people on either of the two life paths in the Sarcee drawing. Apart from that, the similarity of the two drawings is truly striking. Unfortunately, I have not been able to visit Canada to verify the information given to me by Tarbet.

4

The Stone Tablets
of Hopi Mythology

The Hopi believe they will recognize Elder White Brother on his return by the stone tablets that he will bring with him, because they will be an exact match with the tablet (or tablets) kept in safekeeping for that purpose in the villages of Oraibi and Hotevilla. These tablets—one in the care of the Fire Clan and three in that of the Bear Clan—are probably much older than the drawing on Prophecy Rock and therefore more closely linked to the history and origin of Hopi prophecy. While no one is able to say when or how these tablets originated, there is a general belief among the Hopi that the images on them were engraved on—or breathed into—their surface at the beginning of this world by the Great Spirit Massau'u (and, respectively, by Söqönhonaw, the deity of the Bear Clan) to provide human beings with a visible record of the Great Spirit's instructions. We have here a clear parallel to the Old Testament stone tablets containing the Ten Commandments given by God to Moses.

One of the Hopi tablets—the third tablet of the Bear Clan—is in the keeping of Annamae, the oldest daughter of John and Mina Lansa, in Oraibi. To my knowledge, the drawing on this tablet has been copied by only two white people, namely the ethnologist Mischa Titiev (between 1932 and 1934) and Frank

Waters, a writer on Native American cultures (in 1960). Both copies and their descriptions are very similar. Our first illustration shows the copy made by Mischa Titiev (1974, p. 60).

Waters' copy shows no essential differences from that made by Mischa Titiev, except that Waters also saw and copied the reverse side of the tablet, which shows symbols for clouds, stalks of corn, a snake, the sun, the moon, stars, bear tracks, and the Spirit of the Creator—all of which are of great significance in the everyday life of the Hopi.

Waters' copy ([1963] 1977, p. 33) of both the front and the reverse side of the tablet is redrafted on page 56.

It is generally agreed that the lines of rectangles featured on the front of the tablet designate the borders of the land that the Great Spirit placed in the custody of the Hopi when they met him in this (Fourth) world. In other words, these lines express the Hopi's entitlement to their communal land, which is reinforced by the fact that the six figures surrounding the inner rectangle point toward it with their left hands.

However, the two copyists do not agree about the meaning of these figures: Frank Waters maintains that they represent the leaders of the most important Hopi clans, while Mischa Titiev sees them as priests officiating at the Soyal Ceremony—one of the most important religious rites of the Hopi. Moreover, Titiev

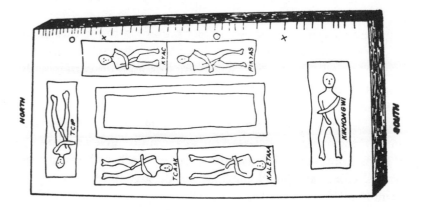

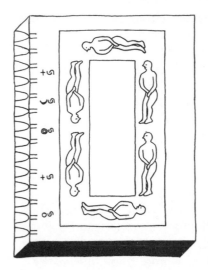 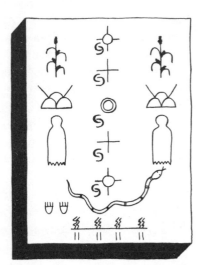

believes that the small signs appearing on the eastern (left) side symbolize the true Hopi way of life.

Their views show that the connection between these ancient drawings and symbolic representations, on the one hand, and the actual content of the Hopi prophecy, on the other, is a matter of interpretation. Without an interpretation of some kind it is not possible to show that these drawings refer to any of the Hopi myths or, in fact, to the Hopi prophecy as such.

The tablet measures 25 by 18 by 3 centimeters and is one of three allegedly presented to the leading Hopi clan, the Bear Clan, by the Great Spirit. The tablet presented to the Fire Clan has a corner missing, and many Hopi are convinced that on his return Elder White Brother will bring this missing corner with him as a sign of recognition.

To my knowledge, the remaining three tablets have never been shown to any white person, although Frank Waters has made drawings of them based on a description given to him by a Hopi informant. Because the accuracy and authenticity of Waters' copies are questionable, it was decided not to reproduce them here.

Waters makes the following comment of the tablet in the possession of the Fire Clan:

> Massau'u was the deity of the Fire Clan; and he gave them this tablet just before he turned his face from them, becoming invisible, so that they would have a record of his words.
>
> This is what he said, as marked on the tablet: After the Fire Clan had migrated to their permanent home, the time would come when they would be overcome by a strange people. They would be forced to develop their land and lives according to the dictates of a new ruler, or else they would be treated as criminals and punished. But they were not to resist. They were to wait for the person who would deliver them. (Waters, [1963] 1977, p. 31)

He further states that "at the proper time that tablet [of the Fire Clan] will be split open to reveal other markings on the inside which will reveal the identity of the Hopi people" (Waters [1963] 1977, p. 300).

Uncertainty also surrounds the question of the exact whereabouts of these tablets, with the exception of the Bear Clan tablet reproduced on pages 55 and 56. In the course of my own inquiries I found that even those who were willing to discuss the matter had no idea in whose safekeeping they were. This bewilderment shows the extent to which the dominant culture of the whites has gradually disintegrated the culture and religion of an ancient native people. Despite this, many Hopi continue to believe that one day the tablets will "reappear to reassert the Creator's promise of peace and justice" (Waters [1963] 1977, p. 299).

The Hopi religious leader Dan Katchongva (1977) has made the following comment on the combined topic of prophecies, stone tablets, and rock drawings: "The prophecies of things to come were passed from mouth to mouth. The stone tablets and the rock writing of the life plan were often reviewed by the elders" (p. 17).

5

How Does the Average Hopi Assess the Traditional Prophecies?

The present-day assessment of traditional tribal prophecies reveals the following picture, which has emerged from numerous interviews and conversations I had with Hopi men and women from ten (of altogether twelve) villages and fifteen different Hopi clans during the summer of 1987.

The prophecies of their people are a compelling factor in the consciousness of the vast majority of adult Hopi. There are, of course, members of the tribe who have not been formally initiated into the adult tribal community, because they either joined the Christian faith or live in cities away from the reservation. Such people no longer have access to the traditional myths and prophecies, which today are communicated mainly as part of the instructions preceding the performance of a rite of initiation. This form of teaching is comparable to the way in which Christian churches instruct candidates for confirmation. On the other hand, numerous elements of traditional myth and prophecy form part of everyday life and everyday conversation and have also been discussed at information meetings, such as the Hopi Mental Health Conferences, which have been held on the reservation every year since 1981. As a result, very few adult Hopi are totally unfamiliar with the tribal myths.

The prophecy in particular is, in one way or another, integral to the everyday consciousness of the adult Hopi. For that reason a publication of the Hopi Health Department has quite rightly described it as "one of the most important shapers of people's lives [on the reservation]" (*Hopi Mental Health Conference Report*, 1981, p. 9). This is true not only of traditional Hopi, in whose case such an awareness is to be expected, but also of those members of the tribe who have made an accommodation with the dominant white culture, as have, for instance, many representatives of the Tribal Council and Tribal Administration. Even Hopi converts to Christianity do not reject this element of their traditional religion but, instead, seek to reconcile the Hopi prophecies with those of the Bible. This pursuit of correlations can reach a point where Native Americans, as with the adherents of the Mormon religion, are referred to as descendants of the lost tribes of Israel (a view that, after the time of Columbus, was also existent in Europe), or where the linguistic similarity between the names "Massau'u" and "Messiah" is put forward as proof of their essential identity.

W.K., a religious spokesman from the First Mesa, believes that the final purification is "just around the corner." He refers to God as "Father" and claims Massau'u to be his son. Just as the Jews are the Chosen People of the Old Testament to the descendants of the lost tribes of Israel, so Native Americans—and in particular the Hopi—are the chosen people of our time. In this way striking admixtures of biblical and Indian traditions have occurred.

Even the so-called progressive Hopi, who identify more strongly with the white man's culture, may, for example, support the mining of coal and other minerals on the Hopi reservation by white mining companies and may use the prophecy to legitimize their attitude. To illustrate this, I quote a press statement that was authorized by the president of the Hopi Tribal Council in 1972: "Our elders have told us that the creator has placed valuable resources for us in the ground and that it is our obligation to discover these resources and to use them for the benefit of man. And this is exactly what we are doing" (Clemmer 1978, p. 50).

Recalling the sources of the prophecy (see chapter 2), we see that some traditional Hopi interpret it in a way that is diametrically opposed to the original idea of caring for the land and its natural resources. In any case, although individual interpretations of the prophecy vary considerably, the narration of its content by most interviewees was largely identical.

Many Hopi, particularly older and more traditional members of the tribe, show a psychological characteristic, the origin of which may well lie in the age-old expectation that one day Elder White Brother will return: they display a passivity and express the hope that help will come from outside. In 1974 the President of the Hopi Tribal Council told a reporter of the *New York Times:* "Our Hopi traditions have taught us that we will be delivered by our white brother" (Clemmer 1978, p. 50).

In the course of interviews, both male and female Hopi have repeatedly stated that they felt "besieged" and "cornered" and that help would have to come from outside. One old man expressly said he was convinced the Germans would have to come and help the Hopi if the Americans deprived them of their land.

The flame of hope for the return of Elder White Brother has been burning for several centuries. This clearly has reinforced a state of mind inclined toward expectation rather than self-help. Or, to put it another way: The *vita contemplativa* of the Native Americans—that is, their inclination toward a more contemplative lifestyle—causes them to be forever the victim of the *vita activa* of the Western Hercules.

The apocalyptic constituent of the present interpretation of the Hopi prophecy appears to rest on a combination of the following elements:

1. A cyclical view of history. Several worlds before this Fourth World have suffered the same fate, that is, destruction. For that reason a periodic purification and renewal of the world appears necessary.

2. The desire for restoration of justice among people. This is

felt to be necessary, because too many persons have strayed from the way of the Great Spirit.

3. The attempt to resolve the confrontation between "whites" and "reds," that is, between Europeans and Native Americans. This requires, above all, that the injustices done by the white people to the red people be made good, that the land taken from the Native Americans be returned, and that the lost balance between humans and nature be restored.

4. The warning that the white people's way of life, because it is materialist and estranged from nature, will result in catastrophe. However, the imminent end (of the world) can be averted, if mankind returns to the way of the Great Spirit.

The accompanying diagram shows the extent to which a central feature of the prophecy has become integral to everyday Hopi life.

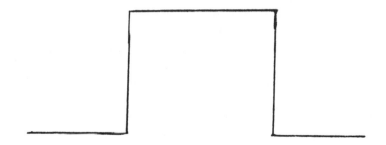

This is the sign with which Hopi brand their cattle, to prevent the neighboring Navajo or whites from laying claim to them. The sign therefore simply means: "This is [property of] Hopi!"

However, the likely origin of the sign is that it denotes the characteristic haircut that is still found today among traditional male Hopi: the hair covers the forehead in long bangs, and it falls on either side of the head almost as far as the shoulders. People of the Hopi tribe say that this "frame" marks the "window" from which they look out in expectation of the return of White Brother. Dan Katchongva (1977) expresses it as follows: "I am forever looking and praying eastward to the rising sun for my true white brother to come and purify the Hopi" (p. 32).

The myth of Elder White Brother has thus left a formative imprint on everyday Hopi life. This can be seen as evidence that this mythologem of the expected savior forms the very core of Hopi prophecy. Once again, it is important to remember that Hopi prophecies are not a separate cultural entity but are embedded in the traditional mythology of the tribe. The prophecy grows out of the tribal myth and is in a certain sense an extension of that myth from the past to the present and into the future. R.C., the deputy president of the Hopi Tribal Council, said in 1983: "It [the prophecy] is all around us, whatever we do—we're the prophecy in motion" (*Hopi Mental Health Conference Report*, 1983, p. 15). L.J., deputy director of the Hopi Health Department, has referred to the prophecy as "the universal knowledge upon which [the] Hopi relies as a guiding force" (*Hopi Mental Health Conference Report*, 1983, p. 12).

These views show that the Hopi generally do not make a clear distinction between myths and prophecies. In fact, the mythical link between past and future frequently is not thought of in terms of their prophecies but rather is referred to as myth, history, "the Hopi life plan," teachings, and instructions. This means that elements of myths about the past are applied to prophecies about the future—projected, as it were, into the future—as, for instance, the idea of recurring worlds and periodic purifications.

Prophecy, therefore, cannot be separated from the body of myths as a whole, because it can be understood and evaluated only as part of that body. In this sense, the predicted purification and destruction of our world is a repetition of the destruction of three earlier worlds of Hopi mythology. And the expected return of the lost White Brother can be correctly understood only by someone who knows that this "return" is to mark the end of the separation between Elder and Younger Brother that, according to the myth, occurred in prehistoric times.

Moreover, the Hopi sense of myth sees developments in time as an "unfolding" of seeds that were present in this world from the very beginning: "Future events have seeds in the past"

(Clemmer 1978, p. 51) and "Hopi myth [is] a process and series of events, whose seeds were sown in the past and whose eventual end may be far in the future" (Clemmer 1978, p. 77).

Such an understanding of the future as the unfolding of a "given" seed literally challenges prophiudluo to provide an integral basis for the understanding of myth. In such a context prophecies evidently are inseparable from the desire to give meaning to the world and to life in general. Whether a prophecy is fulfilled, that is, turns out to be true, can be established only after the prophesied event has taken place. Even in the case of the Old Testament only part of the prophecies are fulfilled. This allows us to take a closer look at the dual nature of religious prophecies. As a rule, they do not simply predict what will happen but also function, at the same time, as a call or warning. Therefore their validity is, to a certain extent, conditional: if they prove successful as warnings and prompt humankind to mend its ways, they no longer need to be fulfilled. Since their warning was heeded, the prophecies have become redundant.

The emergence of human beings in this world and the purification of the world are, to the Hopi, periodically returning demarcations of human existence, beginning and end, past and future. Such cycles reflect the rhythm of the universe—in the case of the Hopi myths, not for the first, but the *fourth* time.

Moreover, that rhythm, like the ever-returning cycle of ebb and flow, implies a periodic revitalization of the human race as such, and this revitalization, in turn, is seen as a renewal of the Hopi way of life. If the white man's materialist philosophy of life gets out of hand, a fundamental purification will be necessary as a precondition for establishing a new world characterized by true Native American spirituality.

Emergence, degeneration, purification-destruction, revitalization-re-creation—these stages become the periodic cycle of the cosmic ages of the world. They form the basic mythological pattern of a cyclical rather than a linear process, a cycle of humankind's ever-present experience of emergence, destruction, and rebirth—as reflected in the rhythm of day and night, the seasons of the year, and human life as such—elevated to the dimension of world ages; it is prehistory's pervasive theme of the periodic death and periodic renewal of the world. And for the Hopi all this is related to the unfolding of "seeds" that have been part of cosmic motion from the beginning of time. In this sense, mythical past and future are one, and prophecy actually becomes a myth for the future. That is why the Hopi can read the future from the past: "We Hopi knew all this would come about, because this is the Universal Plan. It was planned by the Great Spirit and the Creator. . . . So if we want to survive, we should go back to the way we lived in the beginning, the peaceful way, and accept everything the Creator has provided for us to follow" (Katchongva 1977, p. 30).

For a traditional Hopi the preservation and restoration of the world order ordained at the beginning of time are therefore infinitely more important than "progress" and "development" towards something "new."

6

The History of
the Hopi Prophecy

Until very recently Hopi was not a written language, so that neither the myth about the emergence of the Hopi people nor the prophecies concerning the future of their world were recorded in writing, as was the case with the tradition we know as the Old Testament. The only written record of Hopi traditions consists of the drawings on the stone tablets and the engraving on Prophecy Rock. In any case, since the latter dates from the turn of our century, it can hardly be said to be a venerable piece of historical evidence.

The four stone tablets mentioned in chapter 4, one in the keeping of the Fire Clan and three in that of the Bear Clan, are regarded to be very much older and therefore more closely linked to the history and origin of the Hopi prophecy. As mentioned before, the Hopi believe that the drawings on the stone tablets were "breathed into" the tablets' surface by the Great Spirit Massau'u at the beginning of this world to provide the people with a visible record of the sacred directives that he gave to them. There is, however, no conclusive proof that the drawings are linked directly to either Hopi myth or the Hopi prophecy; rather, the connection between the prophecy and the drawings becomes evident only by virtue of the interpretation given to the latter.

In the absence of other written records or graphic representations, the age of the prophecy cannot be conclusively established. Several Hopi I interviewed stated that they had been told of it by their ancestors, who in turn had heard about it from theirs. In this way, that verbal tradition is claimed to reach back to the beginning of this (fourth) world and to the revelation of the Hopi life plan by the Great Spirit.

There was no written Hopi language until recently. It was developed in the past few decades, with the help of Ekkehart Malotki, a German linguist who lives in the town of Flagstaff near the Hopi reservation. This means that in our search for the earliest written mention of the Hopi myths and the Hopi prophecy, we must consult the publications of English-speaking ethnologists.

The first ethnologist to visit the Hopi reservation was Joseph Hamblyn, who arrived there in 1858 in the company of Mormon missionaries. He reports that they were welcomed as the prophesied "White Brothers" but that two months later differences of opinion had arisen among Hopi clan leaders about their genuineness. The missionaries then decided to withdraw from the reservation. Hamblyn's report is the earliest written record about the Hopi prophecy and contains the first mention of what later came to be known as "Elder White Brother" (*Pahana*), whose departure toward the east is described in the Hopi myths and whose return the Hopi prophecy predicts. Since then the question, whether the Elder White Brother of Hopi prophecy and mythology is identical with the "white man" in general, has been hotly debated on numerous occasions and remains unresolved to this day. In all probability there always were Hopi who, even before 1858, interpreted the arrival of the white Europeans—and later, the white Americans—as the prophesied and long-expected return of their Elder White Brother. Such Hopi were, as a rule, inclined to cooperate with the white man and acknowledge his way of life as superior to theirs. For them the right way, the way leading to salvation, consisted in adopting the lifestyle of the white man.

On the other hand, the majority concluded soon after their

first encounter with whites that they could not possibly be the long-expected White Brother, because their actions and their attitude toward nature and their fellow beings were incompatible with the character that mythology ascribed to that helpful bringer of justice and salvation. The White Brother of myth and prophecy may have been an ambivalent figure, but there was general agreement that he would not steal, lie, and deprive others of their land and their religious beliefs. For the traditional Hopi, the way of salvation therefore consisted in categorically rejecting the white people's ways and in carefully cultivating and preserving the Hopi way of life.

The historical evaluation of whites has thus led to the emergence of two factions, which, on the basis of their interpretation of the tribal myths, have arrived at diametrically opposed conclusions about the white people and the right way of life for themselves. A few examples will serve to illustrate this. At the Hopi Hearings in 1955, John Lomavaya stated: "When the [Spanish] Franciscans came, [the] Hopi thought they were Elder Brother, but discovered they were not."

At the same hearing another Hopi, Earl Munzewa, addressed a white administrator who was questioning him as "Elder Brother" who had returned from the East and added, "I am glad that you have found us."

Again at that hearing K. T. Johnson, a former religious leader of the Hopi, who in 1922 converted to Christianity and then burned all the Hopi ceremonial objects in his keeping, compared the myth about Elder White Brother and Younger Red Brother to the biblical story of Cain and Abel, saying: "Those who rejected the white man's way symbolically took on Cain's way; those who accepted took on Abel's." These examples show that there is an undeniable connection between the way in which individual Hopi interpret the tribal myths and their willingness and unwillingness to cooperate with the white man.

These divisions were also the reason for the disintegration of Oraibi, the largest and oldest Hopi village, in the year 1906. Approximately half the population (the so-called Friendlies) saw the white Americans as the long-expected White Brothers and thus were willing to cooperate with them, while the other half (the so-called Hostiles) considered that interpretation erroneous and condemned it as a betrayal of Hopi tradition, culture, and religion. After a determined, yet nonviolent confrontation, the "Hostiles" eventually left the village and founded another settlement some miles away.

Finally, I would like to relate a personal experience to illustrate the divisive effect of the whites on the Hopi's search for the true identity of Elder White Brother. In the summer of 1987 I visited the Second Mesa in the company of a Euro-American ethnologist. As we were walking through the apparently deserted village of Shipaulovi, we suddenly heard from a window the voice of a child calling: "Pahana, Pahana!" (the traditional Hopi name for Elder White Brother). We were unable to locate the child who evidently had seen us and was excitedly communicating his observation to his parents.

Today practically every white visitor to the reservation is referred to as *Pahana*. In other words, the meaning of the term had widened and, because of that, it has become invested with greater political and psychological power.

It is surely no accident that "White Brother" is mentioned in the first written records, dating back to 1858, about the Hopi prophecy. He is not only a central motif of Hopi mythology but a very ancient one that probably predates the "discovery" of America by the Europeans. Admittedly, the Hopi authority Mischa Titiev (*A Study of the Hopi Indians of the Third Mesa*, [1944] 1974, p. 71) inclines toward the view that the Hopi developed the Elder White Brother myth to help them to digest their first encounter with white people (the Spaniards, in 1540); but other researchers and explorers (for example, Richard O. Clemmer and Jerry Levy), as well as Hopi sympathizers such as Zula Brinkerhoff, believe the Elder White Brother motif had its origin in pre-Columbian times.

The Hopi authority Frank Waters is so convinced of this, he has graphically described how the Hopi, in 1540, received the first whites to visit their land as their long-lost and now-returning Elder White Brother. Although the detailed events described by Waters, the initial delight and subsequent disappointment of the Hopi, cannot be historically proven, his description deals convincingly with a dominant motif of the Hopi view of life and is therefore quoted in full at the end of this chapter. Because the Hopi's expectation and longing for the return of Elder White Brother is consistent with humankind's ancient and ceaseless longing for a helper, savior, or redeemer, we may justifiably assume that the *Pahana* motif of Hopi mythology is equally ancient.

The stone tablet motif, too, is presumably quite old, as are the tablets themselves. However, it is noteworthy that the prophecies that are passed on from one generation to the next did not emphasize these stone tablets until after the end of the Second World War. Certainly, the "gourd of ashes" that, according to the prophecies, will be dropped upon the earth and destroy large parts of it is in all probability a more recent motif, as are the three great "shakings-up," of which only two have come to pass. The gourd-of-ashes theme did not figure in the prophecy until 1945–46 and upon its appearance was immediately interpreted as a reference to the atom bombs dropped on Japan. It is likely that this theme is not an original motif of the Hopi prophecy but seems to have had its origin in a Hopi religious ceremony. (Compare Geertz, "Prophets and Fools" in *European Review of Native American Studies 1* (1): 42.)

Several other motifs are also more recent, such as the "house of mica," the "roads in the sky" (on which vehicles without wheels would travel), and the "vast cobweb" that would cover the surface of the earth to enable people to speak with each other over long distances. The same applies to the two "helpers" that will accompany Elder White Brother on his return. One of these is characterized by the sign of the swastika, the other by the sign of the sun. Ethnological literature makes no mention of these two helpers prior to 1959–60. During the summer of 1987 I spoke to several middle-aged Hopi on the reservation who had never heard of them. The idea that the swastika and the sun will play an important role in connection with the predicted purification appears to have been incorporated in the prophecy around 1940—no doubt under the impact of the Second World War—and its first mention in writing dates from 1959–60, that is, the year of the first reference to a red cap or a red cloak that will be worn by the returning White Brother.*

In summary, Elder White Brother and his expected return (bringing with him a broken segment of the sacred tablet as a sign of recognition) are the most ancient and central motifs of Hopi prophecy. Apocalyptic themes (the "gourd of ashes," punishment, destruction, and the expected millennium), the three eruptions that will shake the world, the two helpers that will accompany Elder White Brother, and the imminent purification are generally of more recent origin and a product of what is sometimes called the living mythic process. Yet the traditional Hopi leaders predominantly emphasize these latter motifs of the prophecy in their speeches and written communications. The same eschatological themes have stirred the imagination of people throughout the western world, because the hopes and fears pervading their lives are not very different from those of the Hopi.

We must, therefore, distinguish between the more ancient (and less millennial) traditional core of Hopi prophecy and the more recent apocalyptic additions and interpretations. Originally, Elder White Brother was to bring about the transition of this world into its next phase—since then he has come to be seen as a judge and destroyer.† The original prophecy speaks of only one "purifier"—in the meantime two helpers have been added. The idea of purification was originally linked to the need for a periodic sifting out of what was seen as evil or undesirable—since then, that purification (probably due to Christian

---

* McCelland and the ethnologist Jerrold Levy have pointed out to me that the Bible mentions a savior wearing red (Isaiah, 63).

† Some ethnologists ascribe the transformation of Elder White Brother from a helper into a judge and destroyer to Christian influences: after all, the image of a wrathful creator on his seat of judgment remains an important feature of Christian thought. In the New Testament, too, the returning Christ at the end of time seems to have the dual function of judge and savior, and the "last day" is also known as the Day of Judgment.

influences) has come to be seen as a kind of punishment. The prophecy was originally that part of the Hopi way of life that pointed to the future—since 1947, when the decision was made to publicly proclaim it, the prophecy has become increasingly important and correspondingly independent of the total corpus of Hopi myths and has also been elaborated. At the same time the impact of the white man's civilization on the life and culture of the Hopi since the end of the Second World War has resulted in decisive changes, so that certain parallels between real-life events and the development of the prophecy can be noted. In 1987, Richard O. Clemmer, whose research data was repeatedly used in writing this chapter, stated during a personal conversation that the prophecy could, in this context, be seen as a barometer of cultural change.

Although these transformations, extensions, and elaborations of the Hopi prophecy over recent decades may at first sight be disconcerting, we should not be too surprised at them. There can be no doubt that the transformability of a myth is enhanced by the absence of a written language, that is, by the need to pass things on by word of mouth. For the same reason, it is extremely difficult in a nonliterate culture to establish the exact age of a mythological motif. At the same time, these transformations are proof that a living mythic process continues to be at work. The Hopi were at no time inclined toward rigid orthodoxy or any kind of dogmatic definition of what is uniquely true and therefore must be believed.

The fact that nonliterate cultures do not, as a rule, tend toward orthodoxy and rigid dogmatism could be considered an advantage rather than a disadvantage, because the process of creating myths and prophecies is not irrevocably confined to an isolated past (as in the case of the Christian churches) but part of a continuous life experience. This means that contemporary political, social, and spiritual problems may influence the creation of myths, perhaps with the aim of allowing people to distance themselves from, and arrive at a certain objectivity toward, intrusive events that threaten to crush them.

In the absence of a definite and fixed corpus of Hopi myths

and Hopi prophecies, it is understandable that there can be no single valid interpretation of mythical and prophetic motifs and developments. For that reason, violent and passionate arguments and clashes have arisen among the Hopi (and continue to do so) over whether "the white man" was, or is, identical with the returning White Brother. This freedom of personal interpretation of myths and prophecies has occasionally led to astonishing conclusions. For example, Dan Katchongva, a religious leader of the Hopi, speculated in 1940 whether Hitler might be the long-expected White Brother, because at the time he appeared to subject the world to a thorough trial and cleansing.

Subsequent to the earliest written evidence about the Hopi myths, including the Hopi prophecy, collected in 1858 by Jacob Hamblyn (see p. 66), such data were collected and/or published by visiting ethnologists, researchers, and missionaries in 1883, 1903, 1911, and 1935. In 1883 the American ethnologist Frank Cushing obtained from an unnamed Hopi in Oraibi a complete version of the original Hopi myths and of the Hopi prophecy. Cushing, however, did not publish his records until 1924. In them, Elder White Brother is considered to be identical with white Americans in general. In 1903 the Mennonite missionary H. R. Voth, who spent considerable time with the Hopi, recorded the original myth as told to him by Yukioma, the leader of the Fire Clan in Oraibi. In this version a clear distinction is made between Elder White Brother and the whites. Another record, dating from 1911 and also based on information supplied by Yukioma, sees the whites as possible precursors of Elder White Brother, but not as Elder Brother himself. In 1935 Tewaquaptewa, the then village elder of Oraibi, related the Hopi myth (including the prophecy) to the American ethnologist Mischa Titiev; and the Hopi leader Dan Katchongva told it to Edgar Young, president of the Mormon Church in Salt Lake City. On that occasion Katchongva stated that, on his arrival, White Brother would free the Hopi from all their troubles and misfortunes by destroying the evil ones, that is, by decapitating the "two-hearts." Thereafter White Brother would grant all honest and upright Hopi a life of spiritual and material wealth.

In 1936 Oliver La Farge, a white politician, explorer, and writer, stated that approximately 75 percent of all Hopi regarded their prophecy as absolute truth and even the remaining 25 percent were well aware of it and considered it to be important, although they did not claim to follow it in every respect.

There is no need to analyze the sources in detail, because all of them are, again and again, concerned with the role and interpretation of the White Brother motif. In any case, at that time only a few Hopi, mainly residents of Hotevilla village, felt it was important to let the world know about their prophecy, while the leading representatives from the various Hopi villages had not yet decided to make it publicly available. That did not happen until after the Second World War (see chapter 1), which acted as a kind of watershed in connection with the general publication of the prophecy. The Hopi myth may occasionally have been pointed out to white explorers and ethnologists before then, and religious leaders of the Hopi have mentioned it from time to time, but the general publication of the complete prophecy was consciously planned and promoted by a representative group of religious leaders only after the end of the Second World War.

The Hopi Hearings of 1955 and the Meeting of Religious People in 1956—in addition to numerous lectures, brochures, and communications from traditional Hopi leaders—are impressive evidence of this new policy. The 1956 meeting, called by Dan Katchongva and held in Hotevilla, was crucially connected to the publication of the Hopi myths, because some of the speeches given at that gathering were later made available to the broader public in the form of a small brochure entitled *Hopi Meeting of Religious People* (Bentley & Carpenter, 1957).

I now quote Frank Waters' description of the first encounter between the Hopi and the white man in 1540:

> According to a Hopi myth, their ancestors, upon their emergence into this new Fourth World, were given four sacred tablets by the guardian spirit of the land. One of these tablets, inscribed with

cryptic markings, had a piece broken off from one corner. Massau'u, the guardian spirit, explained the meaning of the tablet and its strange markings.

The time would come after the people had migrated to their permanent home, he said, when they would be overcome by a strange people. They would be forced to develop their land and live according to the dictates of a new ruler or they would be treated as criminals and punished. But they were not to resist, warned Massau'u. They were to wait for the person who would deliver them. This person was their lost white brother, Pahana [from Pasu—salt water], who would come with the people of the rising sun from across the great salt water, with the missing corner of the sacred tablet, deliver them from their persecutors, and establish a new and universal brotherhood of man.

The Hopis did not forget this prophecy when they finally concluded their migrations. Every year in Oraibi, on the last day of [the] Soyal [Ceremony], a line was drawn across a six-foot-long stick kept in the custody of the Bear clan to mark the time for the arrival of Pahana with the people of the rising sun. The Hopis knew where to meet him, too.

If he arrived on time, according to the prophecy, the Hopis were to receive him at the bottom of the trail leading up the east side of the mesa to Oraibi. If not, every five years thereafter they were to wait for him at points along the trail indicated by prophecy. . . . Now the stick was filled with markings and the Hopis kept waiting for the predicted return of their redeemer, Pahana.

Seven years [after Cortez had conquered the Aztec empire], Francisco Vasquez de Coronado, with a resplendent company of conquistadores, marched forth to extend the [Spanish] conquest into the unknown wilderness to the north. Finding the seven golden cities of Cibola to be only the adobe villages of the Zuñi Indians, Coronado dispatched Pedro de Tovar with a small force to the so-called province of Tusayan, which was said to contain seven more villages.

Here the Hopis were patiently awaiting the arrival of their own redeemer and lost white brother, Pahana. . . . All the Hopi clans and kiva chiefs met them at the rendezvous appointed by the prophecy. Here four sacred lines of cornmeal had been drawn across the trail.

The Bear clan leader stepped up to the barrier and extended his hand, palm up, to the leader of the white gods, Tovar. If he were indeed the true Pahana, the Hopis knew he would extend his own hand, palm down, and clasp the Bear Chief's hand to form the *nakwach*, the ancient symbol of brotherhood.

Tovar curtly commanded one of his men to drop a gift into the Bear Chief's hand, believing that the Indian wanted a present of some kind. Instantly all the Hopi chiefs knew that the Pahana had forgotten the ancient agreement made between their peoples at the time of separation.

Nevertheless they escorted the Spaniards up the trail to Oraibi, fed and housed them, and explained the ancient agreement. It was understood by this that when the two peoples were finally reconciled, each would correct the other's laws and faults, live side by side and share in common all the riches of the land, and join their faiths in one religion that would establish the truth of life in a spirit of universal brotherhood.

The Spaniards did not understand, nor were they able to produce the missing corner of the sacred tablet. The Hopis knew then that Tovar was not the true Pahana and that they could expect trouble. It came with more and more expeditions, the hated "Slave Church," tyranny and bloodshed; and these two centuries of Spanish rule were followed by another under American domination.

Someday—and soon—it will be over. The Hopis still wait patiently for the true Pahana and the people of the rising sun. (Waters [1969] 1981, p. 160ff.)

Finally, a German journalist's impression of that long-standing expectation of the Hopi:

Will he still come? Will he find the difficult path through the wearying expanse of the Grand Canyon? Will the scorching heat of the mesa not deter him? The heat of those deserts that look as if the Creator had fled from the scene before quite completing his plan. Has he perhaps forgotten them? No, he will come! One day the leader of the Bear Clan will set forth from his village to the border, which, according to an ancient tradition, was drawn by strewing cornmeal on the ground. And he will extend his hand, palm upwards towards the stranger he meets there. And the White Brother who has ascended the hill to meet him, will return the greeting. He will extend his hand, palm downwards. And the two palms will touch, as a sign of brotherhood, and trembling with joy he will present to the Bear Clan chief the missing piece of the [sacred] tablet, to reveal himself as the long-expected, long-lost and now re-found White Brother.

The Hopi Indians still hope for the return of Pahana, the tribal brother that was separated from them. (Werner 1986)

7

*Variations on a Theme:
The Changing
Interpretation
of the Hopi Prophecy*

In the preceding chapter we discussed the changes the prophecy has undergone during its historical development. The verbal transmission of myths from one generation to the next and the attendant freedom from orthodoxy and dogma understandably give rise to local variations of the prophecy among clans, villages, and, indeed, individuals. R. Clemmer (1978) goes as far as to propose that "there are as many interpretations of the myth as there are individual Hopi" (p. 41). Some central motifs of the myth are relatively stable (for example, White Brother or the stone tablets). Other less central themes, however, have a fluidity that enables them to adapt as part of an ongoing mythical process to the contingencies of the prevailing social, political, psychological, or regional situation. These lesser motifs, therefore, may change, or vary, not only during the course of time but also according to place, clan, village, mesa, and even to differences between individual Hopi.

While all may agree that this world will end, some consider this to be the third of a series of worlds, all of which were destroyed, and the vast majority believes our world to be the Fourth World. Some of the latter are of the opinion that there will be no more worlds after this Fourth World—four being a sacred number—while the majority take the view that there will be a Fifth World, if on the day of purification at least one or two persons are found who remain faithful to the teachings of the Great Spirit. Yet others are undecided on the matter.

Practically all Hopi are waiting for Elder White Brother, who on his return will judge the people, punish those who deserve it, and save the rest. But all these believers are by no means unanimous as to the identity of White Brother. Some believe him to be white people in general; others say that the term refers to the soul, the *I* of each individual—"my other self"— which will return at the end of this world. One Hopi (R.H.) expressed the view that Jesus Christ, who came into this world two thousand years ago, might have been White Brother.

Another (L.J.), who after a variety of religious experiences described himself as "a complete convert to Hopi religion" was convinced that Elder White Brother was none other than the Great Spirit himself. He was called white because he was completely pure and flawless. Everyone would be judged by him, measured in the light of the instructions given at the beginning of this world, that is, the "true Hopi way of life." The people would be pulled one by one by their hair and put before him, and he would ask each one of them, in Hopi, whether they could speak their true language. Then it would not suffice for them to just nod their heads. Elder White Brother would have to be answered in Hopi, since command of the Hopi language implies that one's heart is at peace, for that is what the name *Hopi* means. It might happen that Massau'u would consider a baby to be the only human being whose heart was still completely pure and at peace.

A number of Hopi take the view that it is impossible to say anything about the identity of the "true Pahana," because some consider him an individual, others see him as a personification of an ethnic group or a people, and yet others believe that he is not a living person at all but a mythical being with supernatural powers. "White Brother can be a person or a spirit being" (R.Qu.). One woman half jokingly said Elder White Brother might be the German professor that lived in Flagstaff, who had such an excellent command of the Hopi language, had written books about it, and had helped to make Hopi a written language. (This was a reference to the previously mentioned German linguist Ekkehart Malotki.) The fact that she was only half joking shows what great importance the Hopi attach to the command of their language in connection with the return of Elder White Brother.

In the course of a long conversation another Hopi (M.L.) pointed out that I had made a detailed and intensive study of Hopi culture and religion. When I asked him about the identity of Elder White Brother, he replied that I could be he. Had I not come to the Hopi from far away? And was I not able to instruct those who had strayed from the heritage of their forefathers in the traditional values of Hopi culture and religion? That, indeed, was one of the tasks to be performed by Elder White Brother on his return. This fits in with a statement made at one of the Hopi Mental Health Conferences: "It has been said that through education we will lose our Hopi Way, and when it is all lost, the white man will begin to teach us our culture" (*Hopi Mental Health Conference Report*, 1981, p. 58).

In the course of my interviews I met no one that doubted the prophecy that Elder White Brother would return at the end of this world, although one person I questioned (E.S.) thought it possible that the "end of this world" might not necessarily take the form of a global catastrophe of destruction and punishment. It might be a "transition" of the individual to an existence in the other world, after having led a full and good life here on earth. However, if humankind persisted in its bad and evil ways, the time would one day be ripe for a global act of punishment and judgment.

These views can be seen as variations on a theme. Some older Hopi were agreed that White Brother, or at least the person accompanying him, might well be of German origin. In 1981 I attended a dance ceremony on the reservation. One very old Hopi, after being told that I was German, hesitated for a moment and then said, "Well, you Germans must help us when the Americans come and this world comes to an end." As recently as 1980 David Monongye, a venerated religious leader of the Hopi, in a letter to the Berlin regional group of the Society for the Protection of Endangered Peoples expressed the view that "the great drama in which Germany will play a part, is being prepared" (see Stefan Doempke, *Tod under dem kurzen Regenbogen*, 1982, p. 14). The reasons for these occasional identifications of Elder White Brother (or his escort) with people of German extraction are evident, yet also macabre. The swastika is an ancient Hopi symbol found on many ceremonial rattles, on other sacred objects, and in Hopi art. However, the outer bars of the Hopi swastika may point either to the left or the right. Some Hopi interpret this sign as a symbol referring to the mythologically crucial migrations of the clans; to others it is symbolic of the life force, appearing in the form of a plant that points to all four directions of the compass.

When Nazi Germany chose the swastika as a national symbol, some Hopi considered this to be a sign of spiritual and religious affinity. However, one traditional Hopi woman, C.T. from Hotevilla, as recently as 1987 said she suspected that by adopting the swastika, the Nazis had tried to use the spiritual energy of the Hopi and their land for their own purposes. Others have pointed out that through their discoveries and inventions German scientists have contributed decisively to the development of the present "nuclear" world crisis. Finally, the fact that Germany and Japan were closely associated with the two "violent eruptions" predicted by Hopi prophecy has led some Hopi to accord to these two countries a special place in connection with the interpretation of the Hopi myths. Since the end of the Second World War there have been individuals, and even whole clans, who have felt that Germany, or the German people, had a special role to play in the history of the Hopi people and in connection with the predicted purification. To illustrate this, we quote a statement made at the 1984 Hopi Mental Health Conference:

> One leader, Baasivaya from Shipaulovi—he was about 86 at the time—showed me a rattle with symbols on it. The first symbol the white man now calls a swastika. He said that sometime in the

world, someone would show that symbol. They would be the ones to shake us up twice. They would become very intelligent and invent many things and almost destroy themselves with these inventions. And immediately it dawned on me that the Germans had done this. The Germans had used that symbol and they had been in two wars.

According to this old man, when they had these wars, they purified themselves. And another generation would rise up and would know the true mission of the world, and would stand together to purify this land and life for the Great Spirit.

Then he showed me the sun symbol, and I remembered that the Japanese had used this symbol, and like the Germans they had become very intelligent and invented many things and nearly destroyed themselves. The atomic bomb had fallen on them.

Then the old man said there would be another one to rise up. He would have a red cap, or a red hat or red clothes. He would have a large population and would, again, invent many powerful things and try to out-do others for a long time. (T.B. in *Hopi Mental Health Conference Report*, 1984, p. 61)

To the Hopi religious leader Dan Katchongva, who died in 1972, the idea of purification was "like the mystery of an egg": the egg is hatched but no one knows what will emerge from it, destruction or rebirth.

From this it can be seen that certain motifs of the prophecy are somewhat ambiguous. This also is the case with regard to the role *Pahana*, the Elder White Brother, will play on his return. Most Hopi expect that his actions will be constructive; he will help his Younger Brother, the Hopi, in their need and distress, give them back their land, and make justice prevail. But from another, probably more recent, view he is seen as the "great cleanser"; that is, he will punish the evil ones and destroy all things that bode ill. His wrath will not be confined to the white man, to those who have done harm to the Indians and have taken their land from them. He will also severely test the Hopi themselves to find out whether they still follow the traditional instructions of the Great Spirit regarding the Hopi way of life and the Hopi language.

This can be seen from the following description given by a Hopi elder:

Our old people talk about the day we will all be judged. . . . We will all be lined up in a single file.

Then we will be pulled one by one to be judged. The head priest will grab a hold of our hair and pull us towards him. Then he will ask us, "Are you a Hopi?" We will nod our heads indicating that we are.

Then he will say to us, "If you are a Hopi, then speak to me in Hopi!"

If we know, we will speak to the priest in Hopi. He will lead those who can speak Hopi to one side. Those who cannot speak Hopi he will put on the other side of him.

This is how he will judge and divide us.

Now those people who can speak Hopi will earn a right to stay here on our land for a while longer.

Those that cannot will be told to seek places to live elsewhere.

(*Hopi Mental Health Conference Report*, 1982, p. 48)

In cultures based on myths and characterized by nature worship the ambivalent character of figures such as Elder White Brother is by no means unusual: the Aztec gods had tusks to indicate their destructive potential, in addition to their creative powers; a medicine man may easily turn from a healer into a "black magician," depending on what use he chooses to make of his special relationship with the helping spirits; and the gods of the ancient world frequently displayed contrasting features, such as Janus, the god with two faces, who looks both forward and back, and has lent his name to the first month of our year.

The basis and background of this ambivalent perception of the gods of natural religions no doubt lie in the ambivalence in nature herself: she creates and destroys; she gives and takes away; she is bountiful and lets us starve. A religious spokesman of the Hopi from the First Mesa said: "God the Creator is extraordinarily merciful and extraordinarily cruel."

8

The Common Denominator of the Hopi Prophecy

The last chapter shows that Hopi mythology is completely unorthodox and therefore not given to laying down any dogma about what constitutes a unique religious truth that must be believed. For that very reason the various clans and villages have developed differing versions and interpretations of the Hopi myths and of their prophecy.

When we ignore these divergences and differences and confine ourselves to those beliefs that are shared by everyone, in other words, when we begin to look for a common denominator in Hopi prophecy, we discover the following points:

1. There are two ways of life in the world, the traditionally good way of the Hopi and the way of the white man.

2. Many Hopi stray away from the good path and follow the wrong path.

3. This world will come to an end.

4. The period preceding that end will be a time of disorder, confusion, fear, and suffering. The Hopi language describes this preapocalyptic period with the word *Koyaanisqatsi* (literally, world out of balance). In our present world *Koyaanisqatsi* is exemplified by, among other things, the destruction of the environment, the extermination of plant and animal species, the great wars of the present century, the threat to humankind

of the nuclear holocaust, and the general fear and dread arising from that threat. In recent years a film called "Koyaanisqatsi" has been shown worldwide and so has helped to make us conscious of one aspect of the Hopi prophecy.

5. The end may come soon, because the signs of disorder and confusion are already with us, such as the "gourd of ashes" identified with the two atom bombs dropped on Japan.

6. At the end of this world, a central and powerful figure, who was present at its beginning, will return. This figure is referred to as *Pahana* (alternative spellings are *Bahana, Bohana, Bahanna*) or *Elder White Brother*.

7. There will then be a purification, a time of judgment, and for those who survive that judgment, salvation. The Hopi name for that "Last Day" is *Nuntungk Talöngvaka*.

8. There will be at least one or two persons who have not strayed from the Hopi way of life. They will begin a new world after the end of this one.

9. Because of similar developments in three earlier worlds, the Hopi know about the order of future events. Each of these worlds was destroyed—the first by fire, the second by ice, the third by a flood—because each time, the people became degenerate due to affluence and enslaved by sophisticated technical inventions; they adopted a purely materialistic way of life, deteriorated morally, and no longer respected the balance of nature. From this point of view the predicted end of our world is simply part of a regular cycle of such purifications. For the same reason it is believed that evil will also enter the next, or Fifth, world, so that at some point in the future a further cleansing will be necessary.

Just as their prophecy is an integral part of the worldview of Hopi religion, that mythical worldview is embedded in a cyclical understanding of time. Periodic purification and destruction of the world followed by recreation and renewal are a basic mythical pattern common to all nonlinear perceptions of time. In the Hopi myth and prophecy, our common experience of destruction and rebirth, the eternal rhythm of day and night, summer and winter, birth and death, is elevated to the dimension of world ages.

10. The Hopi claim to know about future events because everything was determined by the Great Spirit at the beginning of this world and engraved by him on stone tablets. The actual occurrence of these events is only an unfolding of something already determined.

11. Somewhat contrary to the preceding points, most Hopi also agree that the destruction of our world can be averted if people return to the way indicated by the Great Spirit. The people would then cleanse themselves individually and of their own free will and so effect their transition to a new world. One Hopi told me, "If we follow the Way of the Great Spirit, the Song of this Fourth World may go on and on. If we do not return to the Hopi Way of Life, that is, the Way of the Great Spirit, then the song of the Fourth World may be very short" (L.J.).

Tom Tarbet, a white authority on the Hopi, said, "I discovered that the Hopi prophecies do not directly predict events but, instead, explain the causes of events to allow us to understand what is happening and what we have to do. That is the most important thing about a prophecy. We are not dealing with an absolute prediction, that such and such is going to happen. Rather, it is a statement about the role we have to play in this world. If we go one way, such and such will happen; if we go another way, something else will happen" (translated from A. Buschenreiter, *Unser Ende ist Euer Untergang*, 1983–84, p. 220).

At the center of Hopi prophecy stands *Pahana*, the Elder White Brother, and his expected return. In a similar way, our attention is increasingly directed toward the Hopi when we think of Native North Americans and ask ourselves what we can learn from them.

In view of this it might well be justifiable to attach some significance to the following associations: North American Indians, by virtue of their culture, hold a special place among aboriginal peoples of our world. The Hopi, in turn, are esteemed among Native North Americans. Mythology is the central feature of Hopi culture. The Hopi prophecy plays a central role within Hopi mythology. At the center of that prophecy we find *Pahana*, the Elder White Brother, for whose return the Hopi wait. There is thus a connection between our hopes concerning the wisdom of tribal people and the Hopi expectation for the return of Elder White Brother.

9

The Hopi Way of Life
According to Massau'u

The need to keep to the "right path," to lead a life in accordance with the directions given by the Great Spirit, is a central feature of the Hopi prophecies. This right way of life is frequently shown to be the opposite to that of white people. The prophecies tell us that after the day of purification only those who have remained faithful to the Hopi way of life will begin a new life and enter a new world.

This idea, the Hopi way of life, plays an important part in teaching younger members of the tribe to lead a responsible life. It is both a model and guide, as well as an example and a yardstick of behavior. In conversations with people on the reservation, the term *Hopi way of life* turns up again and again.

This was also the case at the Hopi Hearings held in 1955 on the reservation under the auspices of the Bureau of Indian Affairs. Many leading Hopi representatives testified, repeatedly employing phrases and formulations that directly referred to Hopi tradition and the traditional Hopi way of life, such as:

"the ancient teachings of the Hopi people"

"these teachings that were handed down by our forefathers"

"the life plan of the Hopi"

"life patterns given to the Hopi people"

"our life plan, which the Great Spirit Massau'u has given to the Hopi people when they came here"

"these teachings, this life pattern"

"the instructions and teachings of my forefathers"

"our life pattern and our religious teachings"

"my way of life, the life Massau'u has given and told us to live"

In this context it is worth noting the following:

1. Again and again Hopi make use of concepts such as "life plan" (in Hopi, *Katsi Vötavi*), "instructions," "road of life," "life path," "life pattern," "religious teachings," "Hopi way (of life)."

2. These life patterns, religious teachings, life plans, and so forth, far from being a product of the imagination, have been handed down from generation to generation as part of a prophecy (embedded in the tribal myths).

3. Hopi generally believe that these teachings and instructions originated with the Great Spirit Massau'u, who transmitted them to their forefathers at the beginning of this world.

4. Rather than being an isolated cultural phenomena, these concepts are embedded in teachings and myths to which traditional Hopi feel bound. This can be seen from the statement that "Hopi prophecy is in reality the Hopi life plan" (T.H. in *Hopi Mental Health Conference Report*, 1983, p. 68).

5. The "Hopi Teachings" are presented in pictorial form on the stone tablets given to the ancestors by the Great Spirit Massau'u himself. Many Hopi have compared these stone tablets to the Old Testament tablets of the Ten Commandments revealed by God to Moses on Mount Sinai to provide the Israelites with a similar life plan in the form of rules of religious belief and moral behavior.

However, such phrases do not convey any information about the "Hopi way," the "Hopi life plan," the "Hopi life pattern," and so forth. In conversation Hopi may frequently refer to their religious traditions, but we are very seldom told what these are. Even Massau'u's final instructions to the first inhabitants of this world sound formal and somewhat abstract: "Now live and never lose faith in what I have given you. Because if you lose faith and turn away from this life plan I gave you, you will be lost and you will later bring trouble upon yourselves. Do not ever lose faith as you go out over this land" (Bentley & Carpenter 1957).

I have questioned many Hopi about the specific nature of that life plan. From their replies and from a study of the examples and guidelines contained in Hopi myths and folktales, the following concrete picture emerges, allowing for certain deviations between the various clans and villages:

1. The Hopi are to live off the land in harmony with it and are to take care of the land and all life on earth. Their land, entrusted to the Hopi by the Great Spirit Massau'u, is sacred, the earth's spiritual focus and therefore the center of this world. It must not be desecrated and on the day of purification it shall be a place of refuge for all living beings. The Hopi were appointed guardians of the cosmic balance and are called upon to preserve this spiritual "force field":

> Our people serve the land through their prayers and offerings. Everything is blessed—the plants, animals, stars—everything that is created. This is how the Hopi earns his place on this world. (A Hopi Elder in *Hopi Mental Health Conference Report*, 1982, p. 40)

> Our first [mythical] leaders told us never to stop carrying this message, that we must never destroy this Mother Earth in any manner. We must never cut it up, we must never fence it, we must never sell [it] to anybody. We must hold on to it the way the Great Spirit Massau'u told us. (T.B. in *Hopi Mental Health Conference Report*, 1984, p. 60)

Because of this concept of a simple spiritual lifestyle, in harmony with creation and all that lives, the Hopi prophecy can be of decisive importance for the environment and for the development of an ecological morality in the West.

At the beginning of this world Massau'u is said to have appeared to the first men as working the soil by the effort of his own hands and nurturing the growth of plants, as an example to the Hopi. "Agriculture is deeply rooted in Hopi religion" (L.J. 1987). In this connection, the planting of corn is considered particularly important: "Whoever demonstrates neglect of land and corn in his or her behavior is unworthy of the name Hopi" (Clemmer 1978, p. 41).

Although the cultivated area of land on the reservation decreases with every year—it is cheaper to buy corn and corn products in the shop—a large number of inhabitants continue to cultivate their plots in accordance with the instructions given by Massau'u. They plant corn and weed the fields; they also speak to the growing plants and sing as they pass through the cornfield; moreover, they are convinced that such personal care and solicitude promotes the healthy growth of corn in these desert regions. Behind this kind of reasoning lies, of course, the conviction that humankind, rather than being lord and master over nature and its fruits, is inextricably interwoven with the whole of life. It follows, therefore, that plants are believed to be sensitive to our words, feelings, and wishes.

2. The Hopi way of life should be simple, modest and diligent. Hopi like to describe how their ancestors came across Massau'u, upon emerging into this world: he was sitting in the shade of a bush, sweating and tired from work. He was resting. In his hands were a planting stick, a bag of seed corn, and a jug of water. That was all he owned. All day he had been planting corn in the scorching desert sun and now he was exhausted from his labors. When the ancestors asked him for permission to settle in this land, he answered: "All I have is my planting stick and my corn. If you are willing to live as I do, and follow my instructions, the life plan which I shall give you, you may live here with me, and take care of the land. Then you shall have a long, happy and fruitful life" (Katchongva 1977, p. 13).

In this way Massau'u gave the Hopi their first instruction on how to live their lives: having no wealth and possessions other than a planting stick and seed corn, they were to follow his example of a simple, modest, and diligent life, with their hearts at peace. This further implies that they should accept the hardships of life and work and be willing to submit to whatever situations arise due to the contingencies of nature. In other words, the Hopi were not to impose their will upon nature but, rather, were to adapt themselves to her needs.

Their very name reminds the Hopi of their obligation to live in peace with each other, because *Hopitu* literally means "the peaceable ones": "Some people think Hopi is just our name. It's more than that. You have to earn that name. . . . In order to earn that title, Hopi, you have to be kind, gentle, truthful, humble and aware of everything around: animals, birds, plants. You are responsible for all those things. And through meditation, prayer and ceremonies you take care of those things" (T.B. in *Hopi Mental Health Conference Report*, 1984, p. 62f.).

However, as mentioned before (see introduction), this ideal life pattern did not prevent the Hopi from becoming involved in warlike confrontations and from taking up arms against each other. The observer of social interactions on the reservation will often be aware of a distinct mistrust, a lurking curiosity, a desire to sound others out, and an atmosphere of resentment, secrecy, and jealousy. There can be no doubt that Hopi society is by no means free from disruptive and divisive tendencies. Their name may remind them that they should be peaceable, but the gulf between ideal and reality is there, just as it is in our society, when we come to compare our basic law—the Ten Commandments—with the way we behave. In the case of a good many Hopi, the observation of a tribesmember that "our everyday life is not in line with our ideal way of life" is all too true.

At the same time there are constant admonitions, such as "we who have Hopi for a name must live up to that name" (H.Y.L. Katsinmonqwi of the First Mesa), or "The last war, or any war, is not the Hopi way. Hopi serves peace. He does not bear arms against anyone. He takes care of one another" (L.J. in *Hopi Mental Health Conference Report*, 1982, p. 39).

Indeed, during the Second World War an impressive number of Hopi were willing to be imprisoned rather than take up arms.

Since then the federal government has recognized adherence to the Hopi religion as a valid reason for refusing military service.

3. The attendance at, and observation of, religious ceremonies and rituals is a further facet of the Hopi way of life. Traditional Hopi society was characterized by religious faith and piety, and at one time men spent almost half their lives performing religious activities. People derived their dignity from the land and from their religion, which were largely identical: "When we feel lost and ask ourselves 'Who am I? Where do I belong?', we find the answer in our religion that was handed down to us" (*Hopi Mental Health Conference Report*, 1983, p. 16).

The careful preservation and performance of sacred rites are inseparable from the religious life of the Hopi, who are now the only remaining Native Americans whose ceremonial calendar remains reasonably intact. In some villages certain ceremonies and dances are no longer performed, because there are not enough people who would take part in them for genuinely religious reasons. Nevertheless, all the traditional ceremonies continue to be performed on the reservation, including the Snake Dance. Moreover, not one of these prayer-dances has lost its religious significance and degenerated to a tourist attraction. As already mentioned, it is strictly forbidden to photograph or tape dance ceremonies, and more recently white spectators have been banned altogether from attending the Snake Dance.

Witnessing such a ceremony is a deeply moving experience. The masked figures emerge from their subterranean ceremonial chambers into the hot and dusty plaza to perform the day-long ritual as they intone their muffled chants, shake their rattles, and beat their drums. The main object of the dances is the call for rain. However, because of their belief that humankind is inextricably connected with the cosmos, the Hopi are convinced that these ceremonies also help other natural forces to fulfill their functions. In this way the ceremonies contribute to the preservation, or, if necessary, the restoration, of the balance of nature.

Preserving or restoring the cosmic balance, which only humans can disturb, points to another characteristic of Hopi mentality: progress and development are less important for them than the preservation of the order and harmony that were "given" at the beginning of our world. The Hopi, perhaps more so than other indigenous tribes, are a deeply conservative people. They believe that all was for the best in the beginning, when this world was created by the spirit beings. And these original conditions can never be improved upon by so-called progress. They can, however, be restored through the proper performance of sacred religious ceremonies: "Hopi is put here for a purpose. No other religion that I know of takes into consideration the whole world, the universe, the unseen. But Hopi does. He is here to take care of the world through prayer and humbleness, through its form of worship. This was the reason we were put here in this life" (L.J. in *Hopi Mental Health Conference Report,* 1982, p. 38).

4. The final and all-embracing element of the Hopi way of life is knowledge of the Hopi language. At times it seems as if command of the Hopi language were identical with leading a proper Hopi life. That is why one of the decisive tests to which Hopi will be submitted by Elder White Brother on his return is whether they can speak Hopi. As has been pointed out, a simple affirmation to that effect is not sufficient; the person questioned must be able to answer in Hopi. Thus the ability to speak Hopi is indispensable for being a true Hopi, being peaceful in one's heart.

We know, of course, that anyone not conversant with the language of his cultural community can, at best, only partially participate in it. To put it more succinctly: "When the language is lost, the culture eventually dies" (*Hopi Mental Health Conference Report,* 1981, p. 23).

At the Hopi Mental Health Conferences, which have been held annually since 1981, no topic has given greater or constant cause for complaint and concern than the growing loss of the Hopi language among the adolescent generation. As part of those conferences, Emory Sekaquaptewa, a lecturer in ethnology at the University of Arizona, frequently conducted courses to introduce the young to the language of their people. Since all religious ceremonies are conducted in Hopi, the survival of the religious traditions depends on the survival of the language. Nowadays initiation ceremonies are often preceded by preparatory gatherings at which candidates are instructed in the Hopi language. In the schools on the reservation, English is basically the only spoken language.

I close this section with two statements made at the Hopi Mental Health Conferences:

> The Hopi language is a vital part of the Hopi identity. Language is inextricably tied in with Hopi ceremonies, customs, teachings, roles, and perspectives of past and current life events. If the language is lost, the culture dies. Yet, despite most people's awareness of the great importance and significance of language and the need to maintain it as an integral facet of everyday life, little is being done to promote its use. As a result, we are at a critical stage where our children are growing up without knowledge or fluency in the Hopi language. (*Hopi Mental Health Conference Report*, 1982, p. 65)

> In one Hopi story it is said that a day will come when each Hopi will be asked to speak by the priests sent specifically to judge the faithfulness of each to Hopi teachings. Those who reply in Hopi will be spared. Those who fail to reply in Hopi will be punished. The survivors, having passed this and other "tests," will be beneficiaries of the continuing Hopi Way of Life.
>
> Throughout the Hopi reservation all the kids speak English. Some speak a little Hopi but mostly they talk in English. Now, some of our elders feel it's all right to learn both languages. Others say we should only speak Hopi. But what has happened is that as we began to learn English, our own native language began to slip away.
>
> This is very dangerous. Our own native Hopi language is very valuable—nothing in our life is conceivable without our language. Those of you who have been initiated and learned the Hopi ceremonies know our Hopi language is spoken at the time. It is the only language spoken in the ceremonies. (R.Qu. in *Hopi Mental Health Conference Report*, 1984, p. 46f.)

Under numbers 1 through 4 we have attempted to describe the central features of the Hopi way of life, which traditionally has been, and to some extent continues to be, a model and guide for the Hopi. To sum up, I quote three more statements from the *Hopi Mental Health Conference Report* of 1983:

Let us once again re-affirm the Hopi values of respect, love, brotherhood and joy, that the Creator gave us to live by. (L.J., p. 13)

To the Hopi, a balanced mind is a mind which relates to all aspects of life: spiritual, mental and physical. The well-balanced Hopi feels himself a part of his land, religion, language and all aspects of his culture—an idea that is difficult to explain to those accustomed only to Western concepts. (L.J., p. 11)

There is no improvement on the Hopi way as an ethic of life. It cannot be improved upon. Take care of the Mother Earth and it will take care of you. Take care of your brother. Take what you need, but not more than you need. Share what you have. Give thanks to the spiritual source of the universe. (Dr. C.H., p. 46)

The traditional Hopi teachings and myths contain no prohibitive injunctions of the kind found in the majority of the Ten Commandments.

When it is said of an old Hopi (such as *Youwyma*, whose name means "Rain walking over Earth") that he had "tremendous commitment and devotion to leading a good and proper life, he was a firm believer in hard work and respect for the Creator and all living things, [and] he lived an exemplary existence" (*Hopi Mental Health Conference Report*, 1982, p. 7), it means that he led a life befitting a Hopi.

10

The Hopi Prophecy
and Other Prophecies:
A Comparison

The basic structure of the Hopi proph-
ecy shows clear parallels with other, including biblical, prophecies. One Hopi woman, speaking of the prophecies of her own
people, went so far as to say: "It is just like in the Bible." The
most striking similarity appears to be that many prophetic
passages of the Bible refer, like the Hopi prophecy, to the end
of this world, the "last days," the "day of judgment."

In the First Letter of John (2:18) we read, "Children, it is the
last hour," and the Second Letter to Timothy (3:1–4) says, "But
understand this, that in the last days there will come times of
stress. For men will be lovers of self, lovers of money, proud,
arrogant, abusive, disobedient to their parents, ungrateful, un-
holy, inhuman, implacable, slanderous, profligate, fierce, haters
of good, treacherous, reckless, swollen with conceit, lovers of
pleasure rather than lovers of God." The Gospel of Mark (13:8)
tells us that "nation will rise against nation, and kingdom
against kingdom" (see also Matthew 24:7–8). Indeed, the teachings of the vast majority of the great religions feature predictions
about the end of the world or other apocalyptic warnings.

The return of Elder White Brother, too, can be compared to
the return of Jesus Christ at the end of this world, as prophesied
in Matthew (24:30): "They will see the Son of Man coming on

the clouds of heaven with power and great glory." Further examples are the Jewish people's expectation of the coming of the Messiah; the promised return of the avatar Krishna in Hinduism; the pledge given by the Iroquois prophet Degana-wida to return from the east in the form of a shining light; the traditional Eskimo belief that a prophet sent by god would come during the night from the east to cleanse the souls of the people and to illumine and guide them. Finally, let us not forget the myth of the expected return of Quetzalcoatl ("Lord of Dawn"), the Plumed Serpent of the Aztecs, who died a sacrificial death by setting himself on fire after promising to return via the eastern oceans as a bringer of peace. Frank Waters ([1969] 1981, p. 162) states in his book, *Pumpkin Seed Point*, that the Quetzalcoatl myth dominated all of Central America for more than a thousand years until the arrival of the Spanish conquistadors in 1519.

The theme of a redeemer, a bringer of peace, or a culture hero, whose return is usually preceded by a great transformation-apocalypse followed by an age of peace, forms part of the mythological heritage of many cultures and religions. The Messiah of the Jews, the Christian's Jesus Christ, the Hopi's *Pahana*, and Quetzalcoatl are all described as "bringers of peace" on their return. They are mythological savior figures, who will return at a time when the world is darkening, approaching its end, and in need of a bringer of light. Such figures seem to be an expression of humans' ancient longing for liberation, redemption, purification, peace, and salvation. J.L., a Hopi I interviewed on several occasions, felt that "the longing for the messiah is eternal." The preceding examples are thus, in my opinion, not the outcome of some kind of religious cross-fertilization but what is known as a universal—a worldwide religious or mythological motif appearing independently in many religions and myths.

The belief that the end of the world will be preceded by certain signs is also found in both the Bible and in Hopi prophecy. Indeed, both sources describe these omens in almost identical language. A religious leader of the Hopi has spoken of "the sky turning black," "the earth turning over," "the ocean coming up" (see chapter 2); and in the Bible we read that "there will be earthquakes in various places" and "the sun will be darkened" (Mark 13:8, 24). The Gospel of Luke (21:25–26) speaks of the "distress of nations and perplexity and the roaring of the sea and the waves" and predicts that "the powers of the heavens will be shaken."

I would like to point out a further similarity between the religious tradition of the Bible and that of the Hopi. At one point in the New Testament Christ states (with reference to the Old Testament) that he had come to "fulfill" the prophecy. In another passage, however, he juxtaposes the tradition of the ancestors with his own teaching ("the forefathers have said. . . . but I say unto you. . . ."). Prophets and interpreters of prophecies would seem to be subject to a tension that arises from their desire to preserve tradition and from the need to take into account the changes that tradition has undergone. The Hopi suffer from a similar tension, as they attempt to fit into the stream of their traditional prophecy and at the same time manifest their individual identities. For that reason, they are fond of using phrases like, "the ancients, our forefathers have said . . . , and *this* is what is meant by that." In fact, the tension between preservation and change is the driving force of the living mythical and prophetic process.

Yet another similarity between the Bible and the Hopi prophecies is that in both cases a former world was destroyed by a flood from which but a few just and upright people were saved. And both prophecies predict that the next destruction of the world will be by fire. It should not surprise us, then, that the Hopi connect this motif of their prophecy to the development of atomic energy by the white man and to the nuclear bombs dropped on Japan. The New Testament, with reference to the future, also speaks of a searing heat. In the Second Letter of Peter (3:7–10) it says that "the heaven and earth that now exist have been stored up for fire, being kept until the day of judgment and destruction" and "the day of the Lord will come like a thief, and then the heavens will pass away with a loud noise, and the elements will be dissolved with fire."

Further parallels are also found in Plato, the Stoics, and certain medieval prophecies, all of which juxtapose the biblical flood with the future conflagration of the world (compare A. Rosenberg, n.d. p. 229). Such prophecies are, in all probability, an expression of our primordial fear of the destructive powers of water and fire, both ancient cosmic elements.

At this point it would seem appropriate to mention the Mormons, or The Church of Jesus Christ of the Latter Day Saints. The name itself has a messianic ring, pointing out that the members of this church, which was founded about 150 years ago, see themselves as "Latter Day Saints"; that is, they are aware that our age is approaching its end, that the last days have come.

For that reason their bible, The Book of Mormon, contains a considerable number of prophecies, such as "And he [the angel] will also write about the end of the world" (I Nephi 15:22), and "But behold I proceed with my own prophecies . . . . for I know they shall be of great worth to them in the last days; for in that day they shall understand them; wherefore, for their good I have written them" (II Nephi 11:11, 14), and "I prophesy to you concerning the last days; concerning the days when the Lord God shall bring these things forth to the children of men." (II Nephi 11:80); and again: "But behold in the last days, or in the days of the Gentiles, the nations of the Gentiles, and also the Jews, both those who come upon this land, and those who shall be in other lands, even upon all the lands of the earth; behold they will be drunken with iniquity and all manner of abominations" (II Nephi 11:116).

Just as the Great Spirit engraved the religious directives and prophecies of the Hopi in symbolic form on stone tablets and Jehovah inscribed the Ten Commandments of the Old Testament on stone, so it is claimed that the contents of The Book of Mormon were originally written on tablets and sealed by the power of the Lord. In The Book of Mormon we read, "And behold, the book shall be sealed, and in the book shall be a revelation from God, from the beginning of the world to the ending thereof" (II Nephi 11:126).

Mormon prophecies are rather elaborate, and I refrain from quoting further examples, because those given clearly show that prophecies play an important role in the Mormon church, quite apart from the fact that its very name constantly reminds all its adherents that they are living in the "last days."

Our next quote shows that the Hopi are well aware of the fact that prophecies are not specific to their own culture but a common feature of all great cultures and religions: "And even in other countries they have prophecies and warnings like ours. And they are seeing them fulfilled just as we are. That is why we must get together and take the spiritual path, humbly within our hearts. We can meditate wherever we are. We can pledge to join hands and begin to work toward getting rid of the things we know are endangering our lives" (T.B. in *Hopi Mental Health Conference Report*, 1984, p. 63).

A well-known and very gifted Hopi artist from the Water-and-Snow Clan, on the Second Mesa, told me, "Every religion has these ideas about a necessary purification; every culture develops forms of cleansing, punishment and illumination." In that context he expressly described the *via crucis* and actual crucifixion of Christ as acts of purification. This artist is not a Christian; he still participates at the traditional masked dances of the Hopi but feels torn between the Christian and Hopi cultures, "like a rubber band."

The traditions of several other Native North American tribes feature predictions about the coming of the white man. As Peter Nabokov, a writer on Native American cultures, points out in his book, *Native American Testimony* (1978, p. 4), tribal legends anticipating the arrival of the white man can be found in every corner of the North American continent. He is also of the opinion that the Hopi prophecy about the return of Elder White Brother is a prediction about the coming of the white Europeans. The main difference between the Hopi prophecy and those of other Native American tribes is that the predictions of the latter have not become anywhere as well known and influential in the world as those of the Hopi. Even members of other Native American tribes refer to and quote the Hopi prophecy.

Despite the parallels among the prophecies of the various religions, there are also frequent differences as to how they are presented. The Bible refers to the Christ returning at the end of time as "Lord" and gives him attributes of rulership: "And they will see the Son of Man coming in clouds with great power and glory" (Mark 13:26). The Revelation of John, which is devoted to an apocalyptic description of the end of time, not only contains references to a "New Heaven" and a "New Earth" but also repeatedly mentions kings and royal attributes, such as power, rulership, throne and sword, military hosts, war and fire, rulers of war, and a king of kings. The Hopi prophecy, on the other hand, presents the returning redeemer as an Elder Brother. In comparison to the biblical prophecy, it is simpler, more modest, more picturesque, less pretentious.

Furthermore, in the Hopi prophecy we find no marked references to false prophets that will appear in the "final days" to lead the "chosen ones" astray (for example, Mark 13:22). In the case of prophecies, which do not claim to be direct and concrete expressions of the will of God, as the ones in the Bible do, the distinction between true and false prophets is less relevant. One Hopi put it very simply: "We'll recognize Elder White Brother when he returns" and referred to the signs of recognition, that is, the stone tablets, which he would bring with him and which would match those in the keeping of Younger Brother, the Hopi people. The identification of Elder White Brother therefore depends on those sacred tablets and the ability to interpret them correctly.

Nowadays, however, the expression "false prophets" is used by those Hopi who feel very strongly that the traditional teachings of their people are strictly secret and should in no circumstances be passed on to any outsider. They explain their attitude in various ways, for instance, by arguing that the prophecies could frighten and terrify people who are unable to interpret them properly. For such traditionally minded Hopi, the "false prophets" are those who have decided to make the formerly secret teachings of the Hopi people public (compare chapter 1 and postscript).

Furthermore, the Hopi myths, unlike the Bible, do not threaten evildoers with eternal torment and suffering; for example, those who have led a bad life must now face an existence of "groaning and gnashing of teeth." There is no such clearly recognized punishment for evildoers in a future realm. The punishment envisaged by the Hopi myth seems to be that those who ignore the directives of the Great Spirit will not be allowed to survive this world.

Moreover, compared to the Bible, Hopi prophecy is also presented differently. The Bible reveals prophets who are spokesmen of an absolute God or whose words are interpreted by religious communities in such a way that God, the Lord, is considered to be speaking through them in order to make his will known to humans. The Hopi prophecy is different, since it is not based on, or derived from, any direct claim to divinity. The prophet is not someone who considers himself the mouthpiece of the Lord. In contrast to other Native American tribes, the Hopi prophecy also makes no use of the formulation "I had a vision." The Hopi formulation introducing prophecies is always either "I have heard it from my forefathers" or "The teachings which have been handed down to us from our forefathers . . . ."

The Hopi ancestors received these instructions at the beginning of this world from Massau'u. For them, their prophecy is not a new revelation or message from God passed on through a chosen human being but rather a future-oriented part of the life pattern and life rule laid down by the Great Spirit at the beginning of this world. From such a point of view, history is the unfolding of that which was originally determined.

However, that which was originally determined is never, as opposed to the biblical prophecies, written down but is passed on by word of mouth from generation to generation, down to our time. For that reason the Hopi, unlike Judaism, Christianity, and Islam, have no theological framework for scriptural interpretation. Instead, the oral transmission of their myths has made it possible for the Hopi to adapt their tradition to historical, regional, and even individual circumstances and situations, thus allowing a continuous mythical and prophetic process. Moreover, because the religions of the Hopi and other Native American tribes do not have a monarchic or hierarchically structured episcopate, in which there is a connection between revelation and rank, differing conditions and lines of transmission have over the centuries led in a very natural way to variations of the tradition itself and to different interpretations of their myths and prophecies.

A point of similarity between the New Testament prophecies and those of the Hopi is that neither of them names a definite date, or point in time, at which the world will end. The New Testament essentially opposes the calculation of times and dates with regard to the final catastrophe. The Hopi go further: they specifically reject the idea that their prophecies ever contained any references to dates or even numbers. For that reason two Hopi (T.B. and D.M.) took vehement issue with proponents of the idea of "harmonic convergence," who had calculated that the New Age would commence on the 16th and 17th days of August 1987 and wanted to quote the Hopi prophecy in support of that calculation.

Nevertheless, the Hopi are prepared to say at what point on our road toward the end we find ourselves, as may be seen from the diagram. This diagram was produced and published by the Hopi to indicate the sequence of the various worlds from the time of creation, as well as the phases of development of this Fourth World. It shows that humankind now finds itself in either the penultimate or final phase of a world characterized by prosperity, abundance, materialism, technology, and scientific progress (penultimate phase), which is to be followed by tribulation (final phase).

The willingness of the Hopi to identify such phases, or stages, on the way toward the end of our world may account for the growing reputation and fame of their prophecy. This is where the Hopi concept of *Koyaanisqatsi* (literally, "world out of balance") enters the picture. The Hopi do not confine themselves

The Voice of the Great Spirit

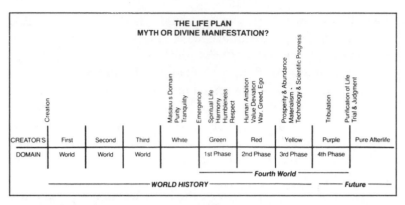

Report of the Second Hopi Mental Health Conference, Hopi Health Department, the Hopi Tribe, Kykotsmovi, Arizona, 1983, p. 35.

to speaking of signs of the coming end. They also describe the stages leading toward that end. The contents of contemporary Hopi prophecy are thus more daring than the apocalyptic and messianic passages of the New Testament.

One final remark. It has been said that it is not the intention of biblical prophecy and apocalypticism to describe future historical developments in advance, but rather to interpret, from a religio-theological point of view, the meaning of history (as leading to either salvation or perdition). This could also be said of the Hopi prophecy and, for that matter, any other prophecies.

11

The Topicality of Their Prophecy for the Hopi

It would seem that the Hopi have always been more preoccupied with, and have attached greater importance to, prophecies than have people of other cultures. Throughout their history they have been inclined to quote or defer to prophecies whenever a suitable occasion presented itself, and this is still the case. It has been pointed out that "the Hopi are very much inclined to 'prophesying' both present and past situations" (Titiev [1944] 1974, p. 201). In many instances, such as disputes over the ownership of land, political confrontations, and even personal difficulties, the Hopi find a solution by recourse to their prophecies. We might say that this tendency represents a kind of search for a higher legitimization of their attitudes and points of view.

For instance, Polingaysi, a Hopi woman from the Coyote clan, spent a considerable period of her life, some of it as a teacher, among white people. During that time her name was Elizabeth White. She always spoke out for closer links between the Hopi and the white people, and at one time even suggested an integration of the two cultures. She maintained this stance after returning to the reservation, where she made a name for herself as a potter and wrote a book about her life with the telling title *No Turning Back*. The foreword to that book ends as follows: "My grandmother, prophetic woman that she was, used to say 'it is to members of Coyote clan that Pahana will come within your day, Polingaysi—or within the day of your seed. And you of Coyote clan will be a bond between the Pahana and the Hopi people.' I am Indian enough at heart to believe that her prophecy has been fulfilled" (Polingaysi-Elizabeth White 1964).

Polingaysi evidently takes the view that *Pahana*, Elder White Brother, is identical with white people in general. Yet it is typical of her to point out in the preface to her autobiography, that the book as a whole, that is, the story of her life, amounts to the fulfillment of a prophecy.

Another example: The life story (*Me and Mine*, 1969) of the Hopi woman Helen Sekaquaptewa contains the following passage about the confrontations between the Friendlies and the Hostiles in Oraibi village, which in September 1906 resulted in the disintegration of that village: "Frequently reiterated during this time was a prophecy that there would come a time when the village would be divided and one of the groups would be driven off the Mesa for ever and that the decision of who should go and who should stay was to hinge upon the ability of one party to push the other over a line which should be drawn on the ground" (p. 67).

The splitting up of Oraibi occurred in exactly that way.

During other political disputes in the past, opposing Hopi factions have frequently attempted to justify their position or prove the "sacredness" of their demands by quoting the traditional myths and their prophecy. In July 1987, Jerrold Levy told me: "All of the conflicts over land have involved people advancing prophecies purporting to foretell the conflict if not its resolution. The prophecies always appear *after* the issue has been around—*never* before. They are always *post facto* prophecies. This has always interested me and I have asked several people why, if they knew the prophecy, they never mentioned it before the conflict or whatever had come to pass. The answer was that their grandfather had said something to them many years ago [when he was still alive] but they did not know what it meant at that time and only recalled it later when it made sense to them."

It has occasionally been argued that the marked inclination of the Hopi to fall back on their prophecies is due to the fact that Hopi society was originally theocratic and was so conservative and inflexible that the only way to bring about any sort of change was to present new ideas in an ancient traditional guilt— that is, to advance a prophecy in support of one's cause in an attempt to sanction one's position through confirmation from the (mythical) past. Jerrold Levy concurs with this assessment. He told me that "there is no way for individuals to make innovations in this very conservative culture unless they can validate their positions with something from the past—a prophecy."

The deeply religious nature of the Hopi may well be one reason why they are so willing to believe in and acknowledge their prophecies. More than anything, however, their destitute lives, continually threatened by hunger from a stony and infertile soil, must have prompted them again and again to seek hope and confidence in prophecies that promised the coming of a helper. Indeed, the very first reports by explorers about the Hopi mention the significance of the prophecies.

In recent years prophecies have become increasingly important in the everyday life of the Hopi. One reason for this may be that after the end of the Second World War, religious leaders interpreted the dropping of nuclear bombs on Nagasaki and Hiroshima as the fulfillment of a prophecy. They were, and continue to be, of the opinion that this world would end before long and thus decided to publish teachings and predictions that had until then been kept secret. These secrets have therefore been freely publicized both in writing and by word of mouth since the end of the 1940s.

Certain critical developments and events within a culture are often accompanied by an increase of prophetic statements. This seems especially true when a culture, and consequently its religion, is existentially endangered and whenever the values, worldview, and way of life of the people of that culture appear seriously threatened. We should not be surprised that such situations give rise to apocalpytic predictions by religious leaders, who extract from the native mythology prophecies about the end of time and/or an imminent judgment, if the people refuse to return to their traditional ways and religion.

The Hopi certainly have been under a cultural and existential threat for some time—essentially since the coming of the Spaniards in 1540, even more so since the arrival of the Anglo-Americans in the second half of the nineteenth century, and particularly in our time. The dominant culture of the white Euro-Americans—because of their belief in the rule of technology over nature, their Bible-based conviction that humans hold a central position in creation, and their Sunday-Christianity—is totally incompatible with the traditional way of life of the Hopi, who did not have even a word for *religion*, because "our whole life was religion" (according to several Hopi and other Native Americans). In our present world it is often difficult to uphold religious traditions. The younger generation of Hopi people may still *understand* Hopi but hardly ever speak it. Most Hopi villages now have electricity (only three have refused connection to the electric power supply) and are therefore exposed to the whole circus of our materialist civilization by American television. The seductive powers at the disposal of a materialist consumer-culture are great and hard to resist, so that even Native Americans, including Hopi, succumb to them. There has been a steady increase in alcohol-related problems on the Hopi reservation, although these are not yet as grave and distressing as in many other Native American territories.

Many Hopi have stated that their culture is being "blotted out" by the dominant white culture, that they feel "cornered" and "under siege." As an example of this we quote a statement made at the first Hopi Mental Health Conference: "The tales of Hopi prophecy, forecasting predictions of destruction and doom, hung over everyone. . . . There is also a strong recognition that times have changed and the old traditions and beliefs are under attack by modern influences. Many Hopi people expressed a fear that their culture is dying and the present world is coming to a close" (*Hopi Mental Health Conference Report*, 1981, p. 13f.).

Arguments continue within Hopi society between the more

traditional members of the community and those who describe themselves as progressive and open to change. The traditionalists often feel helpless to preserve the Hopi way of life, and their complaints over the loss of Hopi values are heard throughout the reservation. The prophecies of their forefathers spring vividly to mind—those prophecies about the coming end of this world, once certain signs or omens are fulfilled. Traditional Hopi feel this to be the case and in their distress are tempted to seek comfort and hope in predictions about helpers, saviors, and avengers that will come from outside.

Although the tradition of their prophecy is ancient, the more recent pressures of the past decades on their culture and religious beliefs have, understandably, escalated the number of apocalyptic prophecies, which, in turn, have contributed to their dissemination among both the Hopi and the world at large.

Many Hopi have come to realize that beyond the threats to their own culture, nuclear weapons and the increasing destruction of the environment are global developments and thus endanger the very existence of all humankind. Such considerations have helped to reinforce the spread of apocalyptic ideas among the Hopi, because they see no great difference between a "threatened world" and the arrival of the "last days." Whether the atom bombs dropped on Japan in 1945 are in fact synonymous with the "gourd of ashes" of Hopi prophecy is, of course, a matter of interpretation; and not all Hopi would answer such a question in the same way. Nevertheless, since many Hopi religious leaders shared that belief, by 1947 their thinking had become increasingly apocalyptic. However, the "gourd of ashes" is just one of several signs foretelling the approach of the day of purification and, with it, the end of this world. Most of these omens are now believed to be with us. In 1968 A.H., head of the Bluebird Clan in Shungopovi village, said, "Many things that were prophesied to us are now being fulfilled."

Those "signs" may be listed under three headings: natural catastrophes, technological developments, and moral decay.

1. *Natural catastrophes.* The Hopi are very much inclined to interpret natural catastrophes and other major disasters such as

flooding, volcanic eruptions, famines, wars, epidemics, strokes of lightning, earthquakes, aircraft crashes, and the like, as a fulfillment of predicted signs. For instance, after the crash of an American aircraft near Detroit in August 1987, in which over 150 people lost their lives—the only survivor was a four-year-old girl—my Hopi landlady (a Christian convert) told me that this was a clear sign of the impending end of the world.

Another such sign is that a time will come when the ground has to be cleared of snow before corn can be planted. This actually happened in 1978 and was reported at the Hopi Mental Health Conference (1982): "Old Man Winter was undoubtedly mixed up, for in late April it was still snowing! An elderly man from Ozaivi (Oraibi) lamented: 'Well, this is how it is to be. . . .' It is predicted that these changes in weather patterns will continue in a more dramatic form and will eventually lead to no harvest with resultant famine and starvation. Another prediction and a prelude to starvation is wind. It is prophesied that devastating winds will envelop the land[s]. One storm will remove prime top soil and growing crops. There will be no harvest" (p. 46).

In anticipation of future shortages and rising prices pious Hopi have laid in stores of food. In this context one Hopi (A.D.) commented on their foresight: "If the supermarkets in the cities were to run out of groceries this week, it wouldn't hurt the Hopi. Because we are ready" (Steiner 1976, p. 5).

2. *Technological developments.* Under this heading there are numerous prophecies, which in the view of traditional Hopi have all been fulfilled, such as people who would travel across roads in the sky in vehicles without wheels. "[And] 'There will be days when one will wake up in the morning, go up into the sky, land at a distant place, eat and be back by sundown.' This is what they used to talk about today. And as I wonder about their words I can only say that those words have come true" (Katsinmonqwi of the First Mesa, *Hopi Mental Health Conference Report*, 1983, p. 18).

Another prophecy believed to have been fulfilled is that a cobweb will cover the earth to enable people to talk to each other over great distances. The atom bomb, considered identical with the prophesied "gourd of ashes," also falls under the heading of technological developments.

Lastly we have the prophecy that the end of the world will be preceded by overpopulation: "Are we near purification? Unless the human birth-rate reduces dramatically or a natural disaster of immeasurable proportions strikes earth or a war occurs, our generation will live to see the complete fulfillment of this prophecy" (*Hopi Mental Health Conference Report*, 1982, p. 45).

3. *Moral Decay*. This heading refers mainly, though not exclusively, to sexual behavior and morality. "Hopi prophecy says . . . that there will be total disregard to clans, your relationships, and even one's own brothers and sisters. Everyone will be having sex with whom they please. We may be at that point or just starting. . . . Sex will be unashamed of. Alcohol will be abundant. We will have our own people laying everywhere drunk. This is what the old people predict will happen, Koyaanisqatsi" (*Hopi Mental Health Conference Report*, 1981, p. 53).

My Native American landlady told me it had been foretold that it would become impossible to distinguish boys from girls, that they would wear the same clothes, that both men and women would frequently change sexual partners, that young people would no longer marry but instead "eat from many pots, one after the other." She felt that all these predictions were being fulfilled and referred to the present time as being particularly hard to bear.

Another prediction mentioned by many interviewees was that if a girl well under the age of ten were to give birth to a child, the end of the world would be imminent. Of those that told me about this prophecy, no one claimed that it had been fulfilled, but all agreed that this would occur in the near future.

Although other Native North American tribes have similar prophecies about the end of the world, the prestige of the Hopi among Native Americans is such that some of them will refer to the Hopi prophecy when speaking of future developments. In 1987, the Tulalip Indian Janet McCloud undertook a lecture tour to Austria to speak about the approaching "End of Our Cycle." After one of her lectures she remarked ominously: "We are living in very dangerous times. You should do whatever you can to protect yourselves, your people and your country. . . . this is the age in which the Hopi prophecies about the 'day of purification' . . . are coming true."

She recommended that her audience conserve supplies in readiness for the collapse of the monetary system. In her view the period of purification had begun on the dates of the "harmonic convergence," that is, the 16th and 17th days of August 1987. She said that many people would suffer profoundly, including the innocent. Finally she advised people to do their utmost to cleanse and purify themselves: "People will somehow have to put an end to this way of life, which is so alienated from nature. They will have to stop all development that destroys the land and pollutes the rivers and must endeavor to lead a more simple life once again" (*Esotera*, February 1988, p. 16, retranslated from the German).

12

The Significance of the Hopi Prophecy for Western Culture and Society

Why should Western society, whose culture and civilization extend back several thousand years, heed a prophecy of a small group of North American Indians such as the Hopi?

Apocalyptic predictions and forebodings of the end of the world are, of course, not unknown to us. We are therefore alert to similar teachings and prophecies originating in other cultures, whose value structure and view of the world are different from ours. In recent years people in the West have begun to doubt that Western civilization has much of a future. Indeed, it may not be an exaggeration to say that Western society, in general, has started to question its capacity for survival. The reasons for such cultural pessimism are many and varied, but we can point to at least four factors that may account for the rise and intensification of our apprehensions about the approaching end of this world.

1. The first of these factors is the acute threat to nature, to the environment, and to people's lives because of the overkill capacity of modern weaponry, genetic manipulation, and in general, the destructive tendencies of human beings. In the spring of 1988, the German-American philosopher Hans Jonas referred to the "apocalyptic potential of technology." In the

light of such dangers, people in the Western world feel that humankind is confronted by a crisis of survival and are beginning to question the validity and rightness of the Western way of life. Not only have many lost their faith in the blessings of progress and in scientific solutions but they are becoming skeptical about technological advances and can forsee the collapse of our industrialized society.

Politicians are no exception. In October 1987, Werner Remmers, the West German Lower Saxony Minister for the Environment, remarked, "This modern industrial society began to doubt the myth of progress some considerable time ago. . . . [and] the old-style consumer society based on ever-growing output has over-extended itself. . . . science and technology have lost their innocence and people no longer believe that our capacity for solving problems is unlimited. . . . we are up to our necks in a developmental and structural crisis." In the light of this he went on to question whether our civilization would be capable of formulating a viable ethic for the future.

In December 1987, Hoimar von Ditfurth, a prominent West German scientist, said on German television, "We are lost. The human race will not survive except perhaps for a very few who may be able to start a new life." This statement about the imminent and inevitable end of our world could have come straight from the Hopi prophecy and would be phrased in much the same way by contemporary Hopi.

The title of Hoimar von Ditfurth's book, *Let Us then Plant an Apple Tree: The Time Has Come*, accurately reflects this underlying eschatological mood, this apocalyptic foreboding. It is based on a statement attributed to Martin Luther: "And if I knew that the world would end tomorrow I would still plant my apple tree today." No wonder, then, that the first paragraph of the book leaves humankind little hope of a future: "Things are in a bad way. To hope that we might get away with it just once more, be it only by a hair's breadth, must be considered a bold expectation. Anyone who takes the trouble to notice the all-too-evident signs of imminent catastrophe that are all around us cannot help but conclude that the chances of our species to safely endure for another two generations are desperately slender" (von Ditfurth 1985, p. 7).

In my experience this passage, too, would be endorsed by many Hopi. "This [Hopi] prophecy coincides with the claims of ecologists and scientists who believe that imbalance in nature has passed the point of no return" (Boyd 1974, p. 51). Both predictions argue the same point: the Hopi prophecy that this world will end because their people are straying further and further from the traditional values proclaimed by the Great Spirit. They have lost their respect and awe of nature and are surrendering ever more to the materialist ways of the white culture. In our society, too, the signs of the approaching end are inseparable from the fact that we continue to subscribe to an essentially destructive philosophy, lifestyle, and set of values: "And when we talk about living in this time when the world is coming to an end, we have to see what kind of world is coming to an end. It's a perversion of life that's being ended: a cancer. Sometimes, to save the earth, some things—that are destroying the earth—have to be destroyed. That's a natural process. . . . When societies become too sick or tired to live, they die" (Steiner 1976, p. 296f.).

2. The second factor contributing to our apocalyptic fears is closely related to the situation described in paragraph 1 and is often spoken of as a "transformation of consciousness," "change of values," or "new mode of perception." Such terms are indicative of a pronounced sense of discomfort and unease about the cold rationality and pragmatism of our social and political structures and the objectification and depersonalization of our lives. Our reality has been stripped of all myth and magic, and the world, of its sacredness. "The new language of *value* relativism constitutes a change in our view of things as great as the one that took place when Christianity replaced Greek and Roman paganism. A new language always reflects a new point of view" (Bloom 1988, p. 17).

All these tendencies toward a new way of thinking—a tremendous and all-encompassing mental reorientation to arrive at a fresh view of our world—are occasionally gathered under the

collective term *New Age*. The movements, philosophies, theories, and modes of behavior thrown together under this heading
are often very diverse and of varying merit. There is no need to
go further into the reasons for the (initially, perhaps inevitable)
sloppiness of such a definition. Perhaps it is simply symptomatic
of the birth pangs of a new era. However, in the context under
discussion it is important to remember that the New Age movement points to the emergence of new mental and spiritual
horizons and at the same time exposes the extent to which life
in the West is bereft of any kind of integral awareness and
holistic consciousness.

It should also be noted that the term *New Age* implies that
something has come to an end and something new is beginning.
Well-known spokespersons of the New Age movement, such as
Fritjof Capra, Marilyn Ferguson, Ken Wilber, and Sir George
Trevelyan, affirm that we are witnessing the end of the old
mechanistic-deterministic view of the world and the beginning
of a new understanding based on holistic-sociological values,
which are similar to those of ancient tribal cultures.

We have here a specific link between New-Age thinking and
the worldview of indigenous peoples and of nature religions.
We sense that our dualistic distinctions between spirit and
matter, God and the world, humans and nature, subject and
object, do not apply in their view of things. Instead, there is an
understanding of the holistic connectedness of all that exists.
For a people holding such a holistic view of the world, everything would be sacred, imbued with the Spirit, part of a greater
Whole, inseparably interwoven.

There is an important corollary here: if the universe is a
holistic network of spiritual energy, it follows that every single
being, too, is pervaded by consciousness, that our small "I" is
integrated in the cosmos, and that human consciousness—
through meditation, thought, and intention—can communicate
and, indeed, commune with everything that is. The central aim
of this revolution of consciousness consists in bringing humankind closer to a cosmic consciousness, a sense of cosmic harmony, and an oceanic awareness of unity.

Anyone familiar with Native American culture, and indigenous peoples in general, will be aware that this new mode of perception shows many similarities with, and "borrowings" from, native cultures. There is in our world a deep longing for wholeness, for the restoration of mystery. The larger world around us is characterized by duallum (since the time of Plato and Moses) and appears to be denatured, demythologized, and profaned. We can further recognize a yearning for a worldview marked by an awareness of the fraternalism of all manifestations, a universal feeling of family, and a sense of cosmic solidarity—in place of the Westerner's traditional egocentricity and the perception of oneself as sole ruler of the planet.

On 29 December 1987, the world-famous physicist and New-Age thinker Fritjof Capra said in a German radio broadcast: "The new worldview that is being formulated now and continues to develop . . . is a holistic view of the world because it places emphasis on the whole instead of its parts. We could also call it an ecological view, because it rests on the basic connectedness and interwovenness of all phenomena, on the awareness that both the individual and society as a whole are embedded or tied in with the cyclical processes of nature" (North German Radio III).

A spiritual transformation of such global dimensions would indeed spell the end of one kind of worldview (and thus also of a world!) and the birth of a new one.

In this way apocalyptic expectations are characterized both by the physical threat to our world and by signs of a transformation of consciousness and a change of values.

3. According to the Christian calendar, we are approaching the end not only of a century but of a millennium (from the Latin *mille anni,* "a thousand years"). This is relevant to the subject under discussion. In English and German the word *millennium* has a chiliastic, eschatological meaning, as it refers to the Christian belief in a thousand-year reign of Christ. This, however, does not imply that Christ's rule will end at the beginning of a new millennium. Humans have always made use of the number 1000 whenever they have wanted to describe

something infinitely great or enduring. The German National
Socialists quite consciously decided to refer to the Third Reich
as the Thousand-Year Reich, the eschatological implication being that it would never end. At the same time, we know from
history that Christians were certain that the world would end in
A.D. 1000 and that the Pope allegedly celebrated a special mass
in Rome at the beginning of the year 1000 to mark the start of a
new era. We may, therefore, expect the approaching end of this
millennium to intensify apocalyptic expectations and to make
us more aware of the prophecies of other cultures about an
imminent end of this world.

4. The fourth factor that enhances apocalyptic thinking is the
science of astrology, particularly its teachings about the cycle of
world ages. According to that view our world will be passing
from the Age of Pisces to the Age of Aquarius during the closing
decades of our century and the first two hundred years of the
next millennium. Astrologers have calculated that each world
age lasts approximately twenty-one hundred years and is
marked by the passing of the spring equinox from one sign of
the zodiac to the next. Therefore, the Age of Aries began
approximately 2250 B.C. and the Age of Pisces, around 150 B.C.
We are thus approaching a further transition.

The Age of Pisces—characterized by love of possessions and
differentiations, imperialist aspirations, clear distinctions of the
differences between the sexes, and dualistic attitudes—will be
followed by the Age of Aquarius, said to be characterized by
human kindness, mobility, nimbleness of mind, independence,
originality, spiritual communication, androgyny (that is, a blur-
ring of sexual differences), peaceableness, compassion, and a
holistic, ecological, feminist, *and* spiritual view of life. Given this
list of characteristics, it is not surprising that people interested
in astrology frequently regard the New Age as synonymous
with the coming Age of Aquarius.

Astrologers variously calculate the beginning of this age as
somewhere between 1950 and A.D. 2200. José Arguelles, an
American student of esoteric matters and astrology, even com-
puted an exact date. On the basis of an intensive study of Aztec

and Mayan stone calendars, he projected the transition to the Age of Aquarius to occur during the night of the 16th to the 17th day of August 1987. On that night, large numbers of people gathered at many sacred sites all over the world to hold vigils of prayer and meditation and to conduct appropriate ceremonies to welcome the sun as the harbinger of the new world age on the morning of 17 August.

Such gatherings were also held at many ancient Native American sites in the Southwest of the United States, including Prophecy Rock on the Hopi reservation. A small group, between thirty and fifty people, made sacrificial offerings, drew astrological signs on the ground in front of Prophecy Rock and, at sunrise on 17 August, raised their hands toward the sky, turning east toward the rising sun, in the direction faced by Prophecy Rock for thousands of years.

It is worth noting that the Hopi themselves more or less ignored these people and their celebrations at Prophecy Rock. Although some North American daily papers and periodicals (for example, *Aero Spirit*, 1987, p. 1) reported that 17 August 1987 was based not only on the calendars of the Aztecs and Mayas but also on the Hopi Prophecy, religious leaders of the Hopi categorically denied this and took great pains to point out that the Hopi prophecy contained neither dates nor numbers. In fact, I was requested to issue an appropriate statement to that effect on my return to Europe. Nevertheless, it cannot be denied that astrology and its predictions about the imminence of a new world age have contributed to apocalyptic expectations among many people and have helped to make them more open and receptive toward the Hopi prophecy.

This is neither the place nor the time to discuss the validity or accuracy of astrological calculations and predictions. The only relevant point is that on the basis of such calculations people all over the world have developed strong convictions about the "End of Time" or the coming of a new age. The flowering of such astrological views is indicative of something lacking in Western peoples' relationship with their world and the cosmos as a whole and that the Western view of the world, based on the rule of human beings over nature and the cosmos, has been unable to compensate for that lack.

While the Hopi are endeavoring to safeguard their own way of life and their order of values, many people in the rest of the world are beginning to feel that the way to secure their lives lies in adopting new life patterns and new values. They and the Hopi are brought together by anxiety and concern about their common future. More and more people throughout the world are turning away from the Western way of life, which is out of control and, in the last analysis, is seen to be destructive. The Hopi want to protect their traditional culture, and Westerners who are concerned about the gathering momentum of unpredictable events are turning to alternative models of life and thought—in some cases borrowed from aboriginal or tribal people—to develop a new, more constructive lifestyle.

A crucial demand made in this context is for the preservation and/or recovery of our lost sense of awe and respect toward God, other human beings, and, above all, creation as a whole. A complete reorientation of the way in which we think and experience the world and ourselves may well be necessary for the restoration of the sacred, of myth, and of magic to our world.

> The Hopi prophecy . . . suggests a way out of our present tragic dilemma. Long, long ago when the Third World became evil and sterile, preparations were made for mankind's Emergence to a new Fourth World. The people were told simply to keep open the *kopavi* at the crown of the head. Through this "open door" to the Creator they would receive guidance to the shore of their new world and then to their homeland during their fourfold continental migrations.
>
> So it was they were led by the voice of their guardian spirit, by *Kachinas* [helping spirits], by a star—by all the voices, shapes and symbols through which intuition speaks to our inner selves.
>
> Today, says Hopi prophecy, mankind is ready for an Emergence to a new Fifth World. Once again we must strive to keep open the door. Through it we will hear a new voice, glimpse a new star to follow. (Waters 1969, p. 71f.)

13

World Ages
in the History
of Western Thought

In the preceding chapter I pointed out that there is a Western tradition of thinking in world ages, the beginnings of which lie in ancient Greece—particularly the writings of the historian Hesiod—or in the Bible, for example, the Old Testament story of man and woman's expulsion from the Garden of Eden. Moreover, the Western tradition continues right up to the present, as can be seen from the works of C. G. Jung and the writings of Fritjof Capra.

In ancient Greece, Hesiod (ca. 700 B.C.) provides the first description of a mythic Golden Age. Subsequently that myth was taken up and developed further by such classical poets and thinkers as Ovid, Virgil, Horace, Catullus, Juvenal, Tibullus, and Seneca. According to it, humankind was initially noble and virtuous and lived in a paradisiacal Golden Age. Then the people began to degenerate, each generation being more wicked than the one before, until during the lifetime of each commentator the apparent peak of immorality and degeneracy was reached. This corruption is described as the cause for people's suffering and misfortune. According to Hesiod the gods first created a golden, then a silver, and finally an iron race. The line of decline is indicated by these appellations and progressively deteriorating conditions. Thus Hesiod and his successors present us with the motif of a continuous decline from an ideal situation to increasingly harsh conditions of life.

However, parallel to those dominant convictions about a progressive decline, there existed at that time an underlying theory of ascendance, based on the idea that human beings were slowly striving upward from primitive beginnings to ever-higher stages of cultural and spiritual development, and that this, too, was an ongoing trend. The Roman poet Lucretius was a well-known proponent of that view, while Ovid, another Roman poet, tried to reconcile both theories by stating that the culture had indeed made progress from primordial times to his own day, that people's lives had at first been no different from those of wild animals, that humans had originally been uncouth and incapable of producing any kind of art. Prometheus, who brought fire from heaven, is the classical embodiment of progressive thinking and ascending civilization. Elsewhere, however, Ovid points to an evident decline and decay of morals and manners. He thus identifies two essentially opposite tendencies—ascendance and decline, rise and fall—each of which is confined to its own laws of operation.

In Roman times a somewhat elaborate application of the theory of ascendance appeared, in that several poets celebrated rulers and emperors of their time as reestablishers of the Golden Age, for example, Virgil, in the case of Augustus.

If we compare these views of classical times to the succession of world ages predicted in Hopi mythology, we find that here, too—despite the expectation of an apocalyptic end of this world—rise and fall, ascent and descent, are interwoven. Both for the Hopi mythology and for the commentators of classical times, each world age is marked by a period of decline, primarily in morality, which then necessitates the destruction and purification of that world. According to Hopi mythology, our present world is not the first such world but the fourth, and the three worlds preceding it ended apocalyptically as a result of decadence. At the same time, however, Hopi mythology tells us that each successive world was reconstituted at a higher level than the previous one, was more friendly and open, and more enlightened. Thus, apart from ascribing the end of all worlds to their moral degradation, it also speaks of an ascending trend from one world to the next. In addition, the Hopi note that each of these worlds was marked by a progressively higher techno- logical development. Their myths tell us that in the Third World the Hopi had already reached our present level of technology and had even made flights to the moon! In each world this technological development and mechanization initially led to material well-being but thereafter to religious and moral decay. Here, too, rise and fall appear to be intermingled.

If we look at the biblical tradition, we find that the Old Testament refers, on at least two occasions, to what could be seen as the end of a world: the expulsion of man and woman from the Garden of Eden brought an end to the initial paradisi- acal state, and the later flood destroyed most of the world while simultaneously purifying it. Only a handful of just men and women were saved. This picture of the biblical flood corre- sponds in many ways to the Hopi myth about the end of their Third World, which was also destroyed by a flood, in order to cleanse a corrupt world. In both cases a few chosen people, who heeded the command of God, the Great Spirit, survived to found a new world.

Again and again the New Testament refers to the last days, the deprivation and suffering at the end of time and the transi- tion to a new age that will be heralded by the arrival of the Son of Man on the Clouds of Heaven. Perhaps the best-known passage is that found in the Revelation (21:1–6): "For the first heaven and the first earth have vanished. . . . behold, I make all things new. . . . I am the Alpha and the Omega, the beginning and the end."

Later, Christian thinkers developed their own myths about successive world ages, as for instance, St. Augustine (A.D. 354– 430) who, in his *De Civitate Dei* (22.30.3) distinguishes between six world ages ranging from the explusion from paradise to his own time. Moreover, Augustine evidently derives the number six from the fact that God created the world in six days. The successive world ages are, for him, a history of God's guidance of humankind and of God's grace and plan of salvation. For that reason they are connected with specific events and figures from the Old Testament, such as the Flood, Abraham, David, the emigration to Babylon, and the coming of a Messiah. With the birth of Christ began the sixth age of the world. The end of our present world age will be followed by a seventh and last. There will be no other: just as God rested on the seventh day of creation, so humankind, in the seventh age of the world, will abide forever in God.

The biblical understanding of time is incompatible with that of the Greeks and the Hopi Indians, who see time as cyclical, so that each destruction is followed by the emergence of a new world. Augustine clearly judges time to be linear, leading from a fixed beginning—the creation of our world—to a predictable end, that is, the return of the world to God. Both views clearly reflect the difference between a cyclical and a linear concept of time, and there can be no doubt that the linear understanding of time, as presented in the Bible, has been central to the spiritual and intellectual development of the West and, thus, for the development of science, technology, and humankind's control over nature.

In the Bible, God alone is the decisive power. All earthly reality has its origin in him and returns to him. In that sense it could be said that the biblical concept of time also describes a vast circle, from God to God. However, the developments along the curve of that circle are linear, albeit directed to the one final goal. For the Greeks and the Hopi Indians on the other hand—and indeed for many other tribal people—cosmic rhythms and temporal events in themselves can be causes of successive worlds, that is, periodic world decline or destruction and periodic world renewal. They perceive the development of the world as circular or spiral. Spring–summer–autumn–winter–spring . . . ; emergence–passing–emergence . . . , and on and on.

In addition to St. Augustine, we must remember Joachim von Fiore (A.D. 1130–1202) another medieval thinker, who distinguished between three world ages, namely, those of the Father, the Son, and the Spirit. The age of the Father corresponds to the period of the Old Testament; that of the son ranges from the birth of Christ to Joachim's own time; and the age of the Spirit will last to the end of this world. These ideas were later taken up and elaborated upon by the German poet Lessing.

In a certain sense, the use of the term *New World* to designate the Americas is symptomatic of the idea of world ages and thus expresses an eschatological concept. For the enthusiastic founders of the "New World," that designation also signified the end of the so-called Old World.

One part of this Old World developed its own eschatology, as can be seen from the doctrines of Marxism and Communism, according to which the emergence of a communist society will spell the end of a succession of different economic phases and the fulfillment of an inevitable process. History shows that Russia, in particular, has always been a fertile ground for lively apocalyptic speculation, as in the myth about Moscow being the "Third Rome." According to this tale, the spiritual impulse of the West, and its power base, will shift from Rome via Byzantium to Moscow, the "Third Rome," where it will reach full and final fruition.

The, by no means exhaustive, list of Western thinkers with eschatological tendencies includes Robert Malthus, who almost two hundred years ago saw the continuing increase in population as the cause of disastrous future wars and famines; Rudolph Steiner, who spoke of a coming "Age of St. Michael"; Oswald Spengler, who prophesied the "Decline of the West"; and Arthur Koestler to whom the mental and spiritual sickness of the human species was attested to by its inability to solve its own problems.

These prophecies bring us closer to our own time, in which the well-known psychologist and mythologist C. G. Jung has pointed to the astrological dimension of apocalpytic thinking. In his later works, Jung acknowledges the idea of successive world ages and speaks of the transition into the Age of Aquarius, which would begin in either this or the next generation. He is, moreover, of the opinion that we are approaching certain changes and reorientations of consciousness, such as occur at the end of a *platonic month* (a world age of approximately twenty-one hundred years) and at the beginning of the next (compare Jung, *Ein moderner Mythos*, 1958, pp. 7–9). In support of this is the statement by another proponent of astrological world ages: "A new historic epoch lasting several thousand years, thus depends on the emergence of a new type of Man, a transformed consciousness, a new way of thinking" (Rosenberg, *Durchbruch zur Zukunft* [Breakthrough to the Future], n.d., p. 10).

The concept of a new world age appears frequently in contemporary discussions about the history of ideas and represents an eschatological notion that is part of our immediate present. It is, moreover, inseparable from the idea of successive world ages, since it links the end of time and the time of transformation to the emergence of a new consciousness, of new paradigms, and of a transformation of values. The proponents of the New Age seek to replace the prevailing mechanical, dualistic, and materialistic worldview by one that is based on ecological, holistic, and spiritual principles. The term *New Age* implies the end of *our view* of the world (and thus of *our* world) and the emergence of a new philosophy (and thus the beginning of a new world). Dostoyevsky seems to have foreseen a similar development: "Now someone is knocking at the door . . . a new [kind of] man with a new word."

In this context, the frequently used contemporary concept of postmodernism is also relevant, because it points out that in art the era of modernism, with its emphasis on what is rational and functional, is coming to an end and is being replaced by a new spiritual approach, which provides more room for emotional, affective, and holistic values. Like the term *New Age* the term *postmodernism* also points to a change of paradigms in contemporary thought.

In Western thought the idea of world ages thus extends from Moses to our immediate present—via Hesiod, St. Augustine, Lessing, Jung, postmodernism, and the New Age. Although our Western understanding of time, being linear rather than cyclical, is clearly different from that of the Greeks and the

Hopi, the idea of successive world ages is by no means unfamiliar to us. Rather, in the history of humankind there is an underlying continuity of basic experience, a kind of archetypal understanding of the world, that suggests that both the cosmos and humankind are periodically subject to necessary and inevitable purification. Accumulated evil is removed and the harmony of original creation restored. In this sense, purification also implies renewal and rebirth.

At least this is true of worldviews and religions based on cyclical time. On the other hand, religions and worldviews based on the Bible, and also the political philosophy of Marxist communism, subscribe to linear time and thus logically claim that the end of this world will be followed by a final salvation, or liberation, and not by another world cycle. (The rarely heard Hopi view that there will be no further worlds after the end of this Fourth World corresponds, in a certain sense, to the latter view.) Yet even biblical thought, as well as Marxism, acknowledges the occurrence of cyclical movements of time in the past: in the case of the Bible we have the expulsion from paradise and world destruction by the great flood and its subsequent renewal; in Marxism we have the sequence of different socioeconomic ages.

Finally, I would like to mention the highly sensitive German romantic poet Joseph von Eichendorff (1798–1857) who, in his novel *Ahnung und Gegenwart* ("Presentiment and the Present"), foresees the end of our world and a new beginning:

> Ghosts are once again haunting our nights. As before an imminent thunderstorm, fabulous sirens rise from the face of the oceans to sing their alluring songs. Everywhere all things point with blood-stained fingers to an inevitable great catastrophe. We are bewitched, intoxicated by our learning; and from this intoxication will emerge a harnessed spectre of war, its face the pallor of death, its hair soaked in blood. . . . Whoever at that time is unprepared shall be lost. For it [the world] will once again go out of joint and an unprecedented battle will commence between the Old and the New. . . . raging madness will throw itself into confusion with flaming torches, as if hell itself had been let loose. . . . until, at

last, the new and yet eternal sun will break through that horror.
. . . the white dove will come flying out of the blue sky and the
tear-stained earth, like a beautiful woman liberated, will arise in
new glory. (Quoted in Rosenberg, *Durchbruch zur Zukunft* ["Break-
through to the Future"], n.d., p. 232)

14

Prophecies in Pantheistic Religions and World Religions

Although prophecies about the end of the world are a feature of the vast majority of religions, their character appears to differ between pantheistic religions on the one hand and universal, or so-called world, religions on the other.

Pantheistic religions are profoundly oriented toward nature, including the soil on which their adherents dwell. Pantheism considers all natural phenomena, from a pebble, via man, to a star, as pervaded by the divine principle: everything in the cosmos is sacred, animated by the spirit, an embodiment of divine energies.

It is unthinkable that anyone subscribing to such a belief would look upon nature as a source of raw material, to be exploited at one's pleasure. Indeed, in the pantheistic view human beings are part of nature, not its ruler, and are responsible for its maintenance and preservation. Pantheists believe that only humans can willfully disturb the balance created and maintained by the Great Mystery and the Spirits, and that humankind alone is capable of restoring that balance. From a pantheistic view, the global disruption and willful jeopardizing of the natural balance such as we are witnessing is a form of suicidal madness.

These basic pantheistic beliefs about the nature of the cosmos have given rise to prophecies that show distinct structural features. The predicted end of the world is no longer exclusively dependent on, or a result of, the deterioration of the people's language, culture, social values, or religious beliefs, but in most cases is specifically and expressly related to the willful destruction of nature, the disturbance of cosmic balance, the declining respect for nature, and a deterioration of humankind's proper relationship with it. This is borne out by numerous interpretations of the Hopi prophecies.

The basic beliefs and convictions of the Hopi are shared by other tribal people. Australian aborigines refer to their past as the Dream Time, a time when the links between humans and nature were still close and intact. They see that the influence of the white people's culture upon their lives has led to a loosening and severing of their close connection with nature. Indeed, their prophecy states that when the last of them are forced to leave the sacred soil and when that soil is ripped apart by the mining companies, the link between them and the Dream Time will be broken forever. They, too, will then be rootless strangers on this earth, no longer capable of protecting or restoring the balance of nature. Then nature herself would fall into chaos.

Other indigenous people hold similar views. In 1987, a Lapp woman speaking about the threat her people were facing as a result of the nuclear disaster in Chernobyl said, "If the reindeer and the Lapps do not survive, the end of the world will surely come." For the Cheyenne Indians, too, the present destruction of nature is a sign of the accelerating end of the world. The Lakandon, descendants of the Central American Mayas, predict that the world will end when the last mahogany tree in the Selva Lakandona has been felled.

According to a prophecy of the North American Ojibway Indians, strange white-skinned people would come to their country, and the life of the Indians would become harsh and dangerous. That crisis was to happen in the Sixth Fire (Age) and came about in just that way. Now the Ojibway live in the Seventh Fire. If the whites were to come again and bring war, they could initiate the destruction of the world. That would be the Eighth Fire. This obliteration Ojibway consider it their duty to prevent. The famous Ghost Dance Religion practiced by several Native American tribes in the West of the United States in the 1880s was also based on a prediction: A prophet by the name of Wovoka foretold that if all the Indians continued to perform this dance, the whole country would become green again, the buffalo would return, the white intruders would disappear, and the Indians would once again be able to follow their traditional way of life.

The apocalyptic myth of the Oglala Sioux quoted in the epigraph to this book is also relevant in this context, as is the following eschatological vision of the Mayas:

> Eat, eat, so long as there is bread;
> Drink, drink, so long as there is water;
> A day will come
>   when dust will darken the sky,
>   when a stench of pestilence will cause the land to wither,
>   when a cloud will rise,
>   when a mountain will be raised,
>   when a strong man will seize the city,
>   when all things will fall into ruin,
>   when the tender leaf will be destroyed,
>   when eyes will close in death.
>   (*Songs of the Tewa*, Spinden & Marriott, p. 62)

The final vision of the famous Teton Sioux Chief Crazy Horse is more positive and optimistic:

> He saw his people being driven into spiritual darkness and poverty while the white people prospered in a material way all around them, but even in the darkest times he saw that the eyes of a few of his people kept the light of dawn and the wisdom of the earth, which they passed on to some of their grandchildren. He saw the coming of automobiles and airplanes and twice he saw the great darkness and heard the screams and explosions when millions died in two great world wars.
>
> But after the second great war passed, he saw a time come when his people began to awaken, not all at once, but a few here and

there and then more and more, and he saw that they were dancing in the beautiful light of the Spirit World under the Sacred Tree even while still on earth. Then he was amazed to see that dancing under that tree were representatives of all races who had become brothers, and he realized that the world would be made new again and in peace and harmony not just by his people, but by members of all the races of mankind. (Brown 1974, p. 166f.)

From the vast number of prophecies featured in the myths and religions of Native Americans and other tribal people, it is impressive that at present no other prophecy is anywhere as well known or enjoys the same authority as the Hopi prophecy, both among Native Americans and white people.

The preceding examples could be supplemented by apocalyptic prophecies from African tribes to show that for tribal people in general, the predicted destruction of the world amounts to a destruction of their natural environment, their tribal culture, and perhaps their very existence as a tribe. For them, their culture and religion traditionally *are* their world, which continues to be threatened by a great variety of influences, perhaps more so now than in the past, due to the continuing expansion of Euro-American culture.

The prophecies connected with so-called world religions, on the other hand, generally pay little or no attention to humankind's environment, that is, nature herself. True, some biblical prophecies tell us that an imminent change or transformation will be preceded by cosmic tremors, or vibrations, but they hardly ever mention the land or the soil, human beings' main source of sustenance—the one exception being the link between land and salvation in the case of Judaism. In India there is the rather abstract Hindu myth of an ever-recurring cycle of four world ages (*yugas*), each more degenerate than the one preceding it. There is also a Buddhist prophecy, dating from 1929, about an apocalypse and the subsequent arrival of a savior who establishes a new and glorious epoch (Willoya & Brown, n.d., p. 40f.). In this prophecy, too, the soil or land plays no part.

Tribal religions, as a rule, have no such global pretensions. For the same reason, they do not send missionaries to convert other nations or people to their view. The way adherents of tribal religions experience and interpret their world in the light of their myths is, in the first instance, purely personal and concerns only the members of that particular tribe in a given geographic, climatic, and historic setting. As recently as 1987 there were still some Hopi who insisted that their religion applied exclusively to pure-blooded and fully accredited members of the tribe.

Because tribal prophecies are in most cases—and decidedly so for the Hopi—inseparable from the tribal myths, tribal people, as a rule, make no global claims for them. The Hopi prophecy was originally an interpretation of the world, the time, and the future of that particular Native North American people. In the course of my interviews on the Hopi reservation during the summer of 1987, several Hopi said they doubted whether their prophecy could have any validity for other nations, white people in general, or the world as a whole. For that reason, some Hopi were secretive and reticent to speak about the prophecy.

However, the decision taken in 1947 and 1948 in the subterranean ceremonial chambers of Shungopovi village (see chapter 1) amounts to the transformation of a tribal mythology into a global myth: the Hopi prophecy came to be seen as a directive for the world. In this context, the global impact of the Second World War and the worldwide repercussions of technological developments, above all the atom bomb, may have been contributing factors. In any case, shortly after the Second World War, certain Hopi religious leaders claimed that the prophecy was of global significance, and they called for the universal proclamation of these wisdom teachings, which until then had been kept more or less secret. In other words, Native Americans and other indigenous peoples are increasingly making assertions similar to the traditional claims to universal validity, often promoted in an imperialist manner, of European culture and the Christian churches.

The Zuni Pueblo Indians, neighbors and relatives of the Hopi, clearly distinguish between what is fashioned by humans and what is created by God or nature, as do the Hopi. One of their prophecies states that "in the end all man-made things will rise against us and a hot rain will fall upon us."

The Old Testament story of the Creation could also be seen as a prophecy—the end could be like the beginning. Of that beginning Genesis tells us that "the earth was without form and void and darkness was upon the face of the deep" (Genesis 1:2).

In religion it is essential to distinguish between prophetic claims and their verifiability. The contents of a religious prophecy are, and, indeed are meant to be, a matter of belief, that is, faith, rather than an object of scientific knowledge. In other words, the veracity of a religious prophecy can never be the stuff of a scientifically reliable, empirical investigation. The future truth content of a religious prophecy cannot be reduced to scientific controversy. This also applies to the Hopi prophecy.

To a scientist, prophecies may be of interest as an expression of a given religious, cultural, social, or political situation. Religious prophecies, in particular, seem to reflect circumstances that signal major cultural changes or upheavals. In this connection the actual prophecy often serves not so much as a prediction but as a warning for people to abandon a perilous or fatal path.

Our study clearly shows that the Hopi are in the midst of an existential crisis. Anyone concerned about the future of our world and the well-being of future generations will readily acknowledge that the Euro-American civilization of the West is also in a critical situation, albeit for very different reasons.

Thus the common concern about the future of two fundamentally different ways of life has led to a convergence of lines that greatly reinforce each other, even though they come from opposite directions. For us in the West, the very existence of the Hopi prophecy, its dissemination, and its recognition should be no less important than its actual content. The growing number of prophets and the increasing openness toward their predictions in our world should prompt us to take a hard and thorough look at the way we spend our daily lives.

Postscript: Hopi Objections to the Dissemination of Their Prophecies

A remarkable number of Hopi are criticizing those members of the tribe who have disseminated the Hopi prophecies throughout the world by their publications and lectures. While these critics do not question the actual content of the prophecies, they make the following accusations.

1. The disseminators of the prophecies are releasing information that is the exclusive heritage of the Hopi people and, in some instances, is part of the secret knowledge in the keeping of Hopi fraternities. A member of the tribal administration told me quite plainly, "The teachings of the prophecy are for the Hopi, not for other people. In any case, the Whites will not survive the coming purification." One Hopi woman even warned me that I wouldn't find anyone willing to talk about the prophecy. Fortunately, she turned out to be wrong.

To put these objections into perspective, I will briefly recapitulate. Native peoples make no claims about the universal validity of their religions and thus have no ambition to spread their teachings on a worldwide basis. This is borne out by the following statements: "We do not set out to convert the world to the truth of the Hopi teachings" and "The attempt to convert others is incompatible with the Way of the Hopi" (E.S. in Tucson,

Arizona). "We don't go around preaching. That isn't our way" (A.D., a Hopi of the First Mesa).

Against that, the proclaimers of the prophecy argue that shortly after the end of the Second World War, Hopi religious leaders decided that knowledge hitherto kept secret should be revealed and even recommended the dissemination of that secret knowledge, because they felt that this might help to save the world from the impending apocalypse and purification. During an interview on 8 May 1963, one of those religious leaders (D.M.) stated, "It is our sacred duty to inform all people about things that have been kept secret from them." (It is worth comparing this last statement with the following quote from the Revelation of John [22:10]: "Do not seal up the words of the prophecy of this Book, for the time is near.")

To this day, T.B. and other disseminators of the Hopi prophecies continue to legitimize their activities by referring to the decisions taken by religious leaders and village elders in 1947 and 1948 (compare chapter 1).

2. The traditional way of life of the Hopi is characterized by modesty, humility, a simple lifestyle, diligent care of the land, and a careful observance of religious ceremony. To make a name for oneself throughout the world as a teacher is not the way of the Hopi. "Hopi was always taught to be humble. Don't be a show-off, don't try to do things better than somebody else, just be humble; self-satisfaction is developed through humbleness" (*Hopi Mental Health Conference Report*, 1982, p. 58).

All these statements undeniably reflect the traditional values inherent in the Hopi way of life.

3. Some disseminators of the prophecy are severely criticized because they accept payment for their writings and lectures and make a living by marketing the religious knowledge of the Hopi people. This is incompatible with Hopi tradition. In any case, because their religion is part of the heritage of the Hopi nation, any money raised by selling secret Hopi knowledge should benefit *all* the Hopi people. However, they have not benefited materially from the publication of their prophecies.

Such arguments may be tinged with a touch of envy. Nevertheless, the Kiva fraternities of several villages have dissociated themselves from the most active disseminator of the prophecies and have severed all religious and social ties with him. More-over, differences of opinion have arisen between traditional leaders approving publication, so that some disseminators now find themselves somewhat isolated from their tribe.

4. It is claimed that those who are engaged in disseminating the prophecy worldwide do so to attract attention to themselves and thereby further their own traditionalist political aims. The publication of the prophecy is thus seen by the critics to be a matter of politics, rather than of religion, which is, in this instance, being misused for (conservative) political purposes.

It is true that the few "publicists," no more than a handful, are without exception more inclined toward the traditional, or conservative, view. For that reason, they are against any form of extensive cooperation with the white Indian Administration. Moreover, they oppose the introduction of Euro-American tech-nological innovations on the reservation, although they are content to use cars and planes themselves. They are also against prospecting rights being granted to "white" mining companies, such as the Peabody Coal Company on the Black Mesa, the border area between the Hopi and Navajo reservations. These traditionalists, descendants of the Hostiles of 1906, consider themselves preservers of the Hopi sacred land, which should not be spoiled or desecrated by open-caste mining or similar activities, as well as guardians of the time-honored virtues of the Hopi way of life.

It cannot be denied that they use the religious traditions and prophecies of the Hopi people to further their political aims. But this should not surprise us. There has always been a certain correspondence between topical political issues and the inter-pretation of Hopi myths, including the prophecies. In political disputes, opposing sides have tried to use the prophecy to legitimize their position, and in many cases discovered such legitimizations. Indeed, in the 1940s the traditionalists chose the prophecy as a foundation for a growing traditionalist move-ment. The Hopi, being a somewhat theocratic society, never

made clear distinctions between the mundane and the supra-
mundane, between political and religious concerns, such as
Europeans have made at least since the Age of Enlightenment.

The progressives among the Hopi also cite their religious
traditions and the prophecy in support of *their* views and
decisions. This maneuvering can lead to the curious situation in
which the chairman of the Tribal Administration will quote the
prophecy to defend his decision in favor of open-caste mining,
while traditionalist leaders, including disseminators of the
prophecy, do so to justify their opposition of it.

5. The critics further argue that the most vociferous propagators of the prophecy are neither religious leaders nor members
of the Hopi Adult Associations. It follows that they must have
obtained their knowledge of Hopi mythology and the prophecy
in a roundabout way, that is, from those who *were* properly
initiated.

It is true that T.B., the best-known disseminator, is not an
initiate, except of the Kachina Society in which nearly all young
Hopi were initiated. The reason for his noninitiation in the
Adult Association lies in his involvement with Christian sects
during his childhood and in his experiences during the Second
World War. However, other prominent Hopi who have made
public statements on the myths and prophecies of their people
have been initiates, such as the late Dan Katchongva (in all
probability the central prophet of this century), Andrew Her-
mequaftewa, the late David Monongye, and others. Some of
them have also been religious leaders.

6. Although the actual content of the *published* prophecy has
not been questioned, it is occasionally said that individual clans
or religious associations have prophecies that are still completely
secret and have never been revealed to any outsider, not even to
Hopi of other clans and associations. In this context, the keepers
of the important Wuwuchim Ceremony are often mentioned.
This criticism implies that all prophecies published so far, whenever and in whatever form, are only a part of the secret Hopi
teachings, although it is not mentioned whether they are the
greater or lesser part.

Their claim can neither be proven nor disproven. If such proof were possible, the teachings would no longer be secret. I am inclined to think, however, that no extensive or important prophecies exist over and above those already published. My reasons are as follows. The Wuwuchim Ceremony is administered by the Spider Clan of Hotevilla. The late religious leader D.M. was a member of the Spider Clan. According to his testimony he has participated in the Wuwuchim Ceremony. In 1987 when he was 100 years old and famous throughout the reservation, he was sometimes referred to as the keeper of the prophecies. He has always argued for the publication of the prophecies and, moreover, has supported the activities of T.B. and other disseminators. In view of his positive attitude towards publication, it is unlikely that he would withhold a substantial part of the prophecies known to him. The same can, no doubt, be said of other initiated religious leaders who have energetically supported the publication of the prophecies.

Our discussion has shown that two diametrically opposed positions are present within Hopi society and, indeed, within other Native American tribes and other native peoples. We have, on the one hand, the principle that religious teachings and esoteric tribal wisdom intended exclusively for a certain group of people (tribe, clan, village, or members of a lodge or association) have traditionally been kept secret and for that reason do not lend themselves to missionary activity. Against that, we have a willingness to disseminate traditional secret teachings globally in order to provide advice, information, and help in the face of imminent worldwide destruction.

The latter position has been argued by the Hopi Danaqyumtewa (J.K.), who connects the Hopi prophecy with the present ecological crisis:

> This is not a message for a certain nation or for a certain person. What I mean is that upright people throughout the world will hear and understand it and they will be united in their will to save Mother Earth and once again follow the instructions of the Crea-

tor. If no-one hears or understands [that message], our earth is sentenced to death. . . . and the last words of the Creator, the Great Spirit, will be: . . . you have ignored all my instructions and guidelines. . . . now I shall take back my Earth. I was the First and now shall be the Last. (Katchongva 1984, p. 29, 32)

Bibliography

Augustine, *De Civitate Dei.*

Bender, Hans. 1983. *Zukunftsvisionen, Kriegsprophezeiungen, Sterbe-Erlebnisse.* Munich.

Bentley, W. and C. Carpenter. 1957. *Hopi Meeting of Religious People.* Hotevilla, Arizona.

Bloom, Allan. 1988. "Nietzsche in America." In *Dialogue* 2 (1988): 16–23.

Boyd, Doug. 1974. *Rolling Thunder.* New York.

Brinkerhoff, Zula C. 1971. *God's Chosen People of America.* Salt Lake City, Utah.

Brown, Vinson. 1974. *Voices of Earth and Sky.* Harrisburg, Penn.

Buschenreiter, Alexander. 1983. *Unser Ende ist euer Untergang.* Düsseldorf and Vienna; Munich (1987).

Capra, Fritjof. 1987. *Das neue Denken.* Bern, Munich, Vienna.

———. 1982. *Wendezeit.* Bern.

Clemmer, Richard O. 1978. *Continuities of Hopi Culture Change.* Ramona, Calif.

———. n.d. "Koyaanisqatsi: A Guide." Unpublished manuscript.

———. n.d. "The Rise of the Traditionalists and the 'New Politics.' " Unpublished manuscript.

von Ditfurth, Hoimar. 1985. *So lasst uns denn ein Apfelbäumchen planzen.* Hamburg, Zurich.

Doempke, Stefan. 1982. *Tod unter dem kurzen Regenbogen.* Munich.

Dumann, Volker. 1987. *Der tiefe Fall der Hochreligionen.* Talk on North German Radio III (22 November 1987).

Eliade, Mircea. 1965. *The Myth of the Eternal Return.* Princeton, N.J.

———. 1957. "Das Heilige und das Profane." In *Rowohlts Deutsche Enzyklopädie.* Hamburg.

Esotera. (February, 1988). Freiburg.

Geertz, Armin. 1987: "Prophets and Fools." In *European Review of Native American Studies* 1:1.

The Holy Bible, Revised Standard Version. 1952. New York.

Die Hopi. 1984. *Informationsdienst Indianer heute,* no. 3. Berlin.

Hopi-Hearings. 1955. BIA Phoenix Area Office, Hopi Agency, July 15–30.

Hopi Mental Health Conference Reports. 1981, 1982, 1983, 1984. Kykotsmovi, Arizona.

Hopi Prophecy. 1988. Japanese film documentary.

Jung, Carl Gustav. 1958. *Ein moderner Mythos.* Zurich.

Kaiser, Rudolf. 1985. *Gesang des Regenbogens: Indianische Gebete.* Münster.

———. 1986. "This Land Is Sacred: Views and Values of North American Indians." In *Arbeitsmittel für die Sekundarstufe II, Englisch.* Hannover.

———. 1987. "Chief Seattle's Speech(es): American Origins and European Reception." In *Recovering the Word: Essays on Native American Literature,* edited by Brian Swann and Arnold Krupat, 497–536. Berkeley, Calif.

———. 1987. *Dies sind meine Worte: Indianische Häuptlingsreden.* Münster.

———. 1987. Field notes.

———. 1987 "A Fifth Gospel, Almost: Chief Seattle's Speeches." In *Indians and Europe: An Interdisciplinary Collection of Essays,* edited by Christian F. Feest, 505–526. Aachen, Germany.

Kaiser, Rudolf, and Michaela Kaiser. 1984, 1986. *Diese Erde ist uns heilig: Die Rede des Indianerhäuptlings Seattle, Legende und Wirklichkeit.* Münster.

———. 1984. *Sonnenfänger: Indianische Texte.* Münster.

Katchongva, Dan. 1977. *From the Beginning of Life to the Day of Purification.* Los Angeles.

———. 1984. Hopi: "Eine indianische Botschaft." *CH-4303 Kaiseraugst.* Agna Incomindios.

Nabokov, Peter. 1978. *Native American Testimony.* New York.

Polingaysi (Elizabeth White). 1964. *No Turning Back.* Albuquerque, N.M.

Powers, William K. 1977. *Oglala Religion*. Lincoln, Nebraska.

Rahner, Karl. 1958. *Visionen und Prophezeiungen*. Freiburg.

Remmers, Werner. 1987. "CDU-Programmatik in der säkularisierten Wohlstandsgesellschaft." In *Sonde* 3/4 (October 1987).

Rohr, Daniel C. 1985. "Alles, was ich habe, ist mein Pflanzstock und mein Mais." *CH-4303 Kaiseraugst*. Agna Incomindios.

Rosenberg, Alfons. n.d.: *Durchbruch zur Zukunft*. Bietigheim, Württemberg.

Sekaquaptewa, Helen. 1969. *Me and Mine*. Tucson, Ariz.

Smith, Martin Cruz. 1982. *Flügel der Nacht*. Frankfurt, Berlin, Vienna.

Spinden, H. J. and A. Marriott. [1933] 1976. *Songs of the Tewa*. Santa Fe, N.M.

Steiner, Stan. 1976. *The Vanishing White Man*. New York.

Tarbet, Tom. 1981. *The Essence of Hopi Prophecy*. Santa Fe, N.M.

Titiev, Mischa. [1944] 1974. *A Study of Hopi Indians of Third Mesa*. Cambridge, Mass.

Waters, Frank. [1963] 1977. *Book of the Hopi*. New York.

———. [1969] 1981. *Pumpkin Seed Point*. Athens, Ohio and Chicago.

———. 1977. "The Hopi Prophecy and the Chinese Dream," in *East-West* (May 1977).

Werner, Jürgen. 1986. "Die Welt der Edlen Wilden." In *FAZ-Magazin* no. 311, pp. 34–45.

Willoya, William, and Vinson Brown. n.d. *Warriors of the Rainbow*. Healdsburg, Calif.